Message Sent

*Retrieving
the
Gift of Love*

"Terri's book touched me so deeply. I am a therapist that has counseled people for over 15 years. These writings have been a guide in helping me understand how I am affected and internalize others' behaviors and actions. *Message Sent* has helped me with interactions amongst friends. I feel it has helped me understand and be in a place I need to be for my children. Terri's book has also been a guide and an answer to struggles regarding my upbringing, and has been a key factor in working through a traumatic event that could have held me back in my path to life happiness. This book can help me in just about any area of my life. *Message Sent* is the nicest gift I can give to others."

—Mary Foland, L.C.S.W.

"*Message Sent* touches your heart at a very personal level. Terri takes you on her own voyage of self-discovery and challenges you to do the same. As you examine your own spiritual truth, your life is transformed in monumental ways! I highly recommend this book."

—Greg Fowler, Tennis Instructor

"This book kept me glued to my chair for days. I couldn't put it down. Each story reflected something in my life that needed healing. I love that *Message Sent* helped me to look honestly at myself, bringing awareness to my wounds, and that it was able to give me the tools to aid in healing. As a result, it has helped me achieve self-love and acceptance."

—Barbara Watts, R.N.

"*Message Sent* reminded me of what is most important in life, unconditional love, and helped me move closer towards reaching that goal. I found that by doing the lessons, I was able to slow down and retain more from each of them and, thus, integrate what I learned more easily into my life. The individual and family lessons allowed me to look at my life and helped me create more meaningful discussions with my wife that improved our communication and brought us closer together."

—David Reynolds, Business Professional

Message Sent

Retrieving
the
Gift of Love

Terri Amos

WorldofLite Publishing

Cover design by Robert Aulicino
Cover photograph of the author by Bader Howar

For inquiries, please contact:
WorldofLite Publishing
2110 Artesia Blvd., #B 273
Redondo Beach, CA 90278-3069

E-mail: worldoflite@aol.com

Printed in the United States of America

Publisher's Cataloging-in-Publication
(Provided by Quaity Books, Inc.)

Amos, Terri.
   Message sent : retrieving the gift of love / Terri Amos.
   p. cm.
   LCCN 2002104459
   ISBN 0-9719694-0-X

   1. Self-actualization (Psychology)
   2. Self-realization. 3. Spiritual life. 4. Meditation

BF637.S4A46 2002   158.1
                    QB102-701497

To my husband,
Steve

And
To my children,
A.J.
Mackenzie
&
Kolbi

I love you all.
You are God's gifts to me.

Contents

Acknowledgments

First and foremost in my life is my relationship with God. I am so thankful that the love I have learned to trust is always there. Thank you, God.

To my husband, Steve, there are no words to say how much I love you and how much I appreciate your support. You have always believed in me. Thank you for your consistency and undying love. I love you.

I am so thankful for my children, A.J., Mackenzie, and Kolbi. I truly feel you are God's angels sent down to guide me on my path. Thank you for being my inspiration.

To my mom and dad, Lee and Keith Utley, thank you for loving me and doing your very best. Mom, I thank you for continually stretching your boundaries to love and support me. And, Dad, even though you have passed on, the seed you planted many years ago continues to grow. You told me I could be anything I wanted to be. Well, I finally believe! Thank you.

To my sister, Kelly Caldwell, thank you for being you and for standing in your truth, which, in turn, helped me to find mine.

Erlinda Cruz, you are my right arm. I don't know what I would have done without you all these years. Thank you.

I have been blessed with dear friends who have supported me throughout this healing process. Renee Mulcahy, Linda Georgouses, Barbara Watts, Patty Kamson, and Ruth Romero, you are all so very special to me. Renee, you stretch my boundaries. Linda, you always laugh and cry with me. Barbara, for many years you have consistently loved and supported me. Patty, your words of wisdom soothe me and guide me. And, Ruth, you've always loved me and inspired me. Each one of you is so special and unique. I thank you from the bottom of my heart for being such wonderful friends.

To Mary Foland, I would like to say a great big thank you. You were the first to read my book. In what could have been a very scary experience for me, you filled me with love and became an inspiration. Thank you.

Greg Fowler and David Reynolds, I thank you both for being so courageous and for supporting my work and me. Thank you.

To all of the people in this book whose names were changed or not given, you have helped me down my path to wholeness. Thank you.

As I began my healing journey, I prayed for a kind and gentle teacher. My prayers were answered with Judy Nelson of Clearsight, a school for energetic and spiritual healing and the development of intuitive skills, located in Santa Monica, California. Thank you, Judy, for being you and for the many wonderful tools you taught me, including some that are in this book.

And to Dr. Arthur Mikaelian, you guided me into a whole new level of learning and understanding. Thank you for everything!

There are people who I have never met and, yet, inspired me along the way. Neale Donald Walsch, you stood in your truth with your *Conversations with God* books. By doing this, you planted the seed for me to do the same. Thank you.

And to Cheryl Richardson, I heard you speak several years ago at an expo. You are the one who said to prioritize your life. I did and now look what I've done! I've made time to heal and time to write this book. Thank you!

Now a big thank you to the "ABC Team." These are the people who have come into my life to "accelerate my book and career."

First, I am in great gratitude to Cheri Ingram. Cheri, I don't know where you came from, but I tend to believe you were an angel sitting on a cloud up above waiting for my signal to come. When I didn't know which way to turn with my book and career, I prayed for help, and then you appeared. Thank you for everything!

Sandy Holst, you have been terrific as a mentor and a friend. Thank you for your support and allowing me to grace the pages of your book, *A Special Moment in Your Life*. God bless you.

Bob Aulicino, you are a pleasure to work with and did a fantastic job designing this book. Thank you for your hard work and flexibility.

Mary Embree of Embree Literary Services, I can't begin to tell you how much your help has meant to me. Thank you for everything, including creating the copy on the back cover of this book.

And to Bill Frank, thank you for your guidance. You are an angel!

To Chuck Mitchell, thank you for telling me years ago that I should write and then for guiding me to the man who edited *Message Sent*.

That leads me to Robert Windeler. Robert, thank you for helping with the editing process. The first time is never easy. But, because of you, I grew deeper in my truth and, as a result, became a better writer. Thank you!

To Marco Vibal, I thank you for your expert eyes, your enthusiasm, and your desire to help out with proofreading this book. Thank you.

Bader Howar, you are an amazing photographer! Thank you for your brilliance and for the wonderful picture on the cover of this book.

Thank you to the team who made me look so good the

day of my photo shoot. I know I will never look quite the same. David Blair, Keith Crary, and John McCormick, you are all masters with your work. Thank you.

And to Luke and Rona O'Connor of Lukaro Salon in Beverly Hills, I thank you both. You two have been such a supportive team to me over the years. Thank you for your friendship and for always helping me look my best.

Amy Cook of Visionseeker.org and Ruben Perez, thank you for terriamos.com. You gave me a fabulous avenue to get my message out into the world. Thank you!

To each of the people I have mentioned here, you have touched my soul so very deeply. There are no words to describe how much your presence in my life means to me. Thank you all.

And last, but definitely not least, I want to say thank you to you, the reader. By reading this book you are making a commitment to healing and standing in your truth. Thank you for being a light unto the darkness. Thank you for being you!

—Terri Amos

I am a spiritual warrior
I stand for truth and integrity
I stand for being who I am
Living from my heart and what I believe
No other person's judgment shall hurt me
For God is my authority
This is who I am

Introduction

I am weeping tears of confusion. I have just been named Miss U.S.A. of 1982. The audience is whistling and yelling. Their applause thunders through my brain. The crowd seems thrilled that this little girl from Arkansas is wearing the glittery crown atop her short brown mane.

But I am not finding a whole lot of joy in this moment. Even Bob Barker, the host of the pageant, says, "Terri Utley, show everyone how happy you are." He can see my face. It has a look of dread.

"What have I done to my life? Is this what I anticipated? Then why am I so confused?" These questions race through my mind. The competitive side of me is thrilled to have won. And, yet, there is a lack I can't describe. My confusion surfaces because there is an emptiness inside me. That's because the love has come from the outside, rather than from within me. At this time, the spring of 1982, I don't comprehend this, but later I do. I can see clearly now, because I've opened up to my truth.

I spent my whole life seeking others' approval. And to be quite honest, I often got it. I constantly sought out the next achievement that I could hang on my wall or put in my scrapbook. I was the perfect picture of what a young woman should be, at least most of the time. But this was only on the outside. On the inside I was dying…dying from anger and pain.

The problem was that I didn't love me. I constantly judged myself, never letting my mind take a rest. I thought I had to be perfect…I thought I had to be best. I never forgave myself. And because I couldn't forgive me, I couldn't forgive anyone else.

The anger raged inside of me. It was like a beast that I couldn't tame. Most of the time I held it back, until I became so enraged that I had to attack. My victims were the people around me. I expressed my anger through control and hate, and sometimes with a fist or a slap. I expressed it because I denied my pain.

The source of my pain was simple. I had denied the true me. I wouldn't allow myself to be human, for fear that no one would accept or love me.

Fear ran rampant through my soul. I was afraid of being judged. I was afraid I wasn't good enough to be loved. Fear kept me in control…control of anything and everything in the world around me.

This control carried over to my family. When I married my husband, Steve, he came with a ready-made family. His son, A.J., who is now a young adult, was just turning five when I entered his life. I often found myself screaming at A.J. I thought I had to make him "the best" for the world to see.

A.J. says one of his most vivid memories was when I made him write the word "yes" a hundred times because he had said "yeah" one too many times for me. The only thing this created was more anxiety for the whole family. I remember crouching down on my knees next to A.J.'s bedside, sobbing, "I don't know how to love you!" I hated myself for being this way. I knew I was affecting this child and causing him great pain. What I really wanted in my heart was to love A.J. unconditionally and for my family to feel whole. I didn't know how to love him, though, because I was stuck in limiting societal beliefs and wouldn't allow him, or myself, to live authentically. The pain, frustration and anger only continued as our girls, Mackenzie and Kolbi, were born.

Then life presented me a beautiful gift…the gift of change. I discovered I didn't have to be this way. I had a choice. I didn't exercise this choice, however, until my dad died in

January 1995. That's when I truly woke up and began to heal my life.

When Daddy died he left me with one of the greatest gifts of my life. I loved him so much, but knew I did not want to be like him. He had become very separate from the world because he saw himself as a failure. He had lost everything in bankruptcy and his life had turned upside down. In his mind, he had to create the perfect life for all to see, and he had failed at it. He thought perfection would win him approval in life. I thought the same thing. That is until I saw him die a broken man. We tried to tell Dad that nothing mattered but him and we loved him, but he couldn't hear it. He was stuck under the mud of his life and couldn't see any light. He was the grand judge and jury and I learned how to be that from watching him. When he died and I saw how shut down he had become, I knew I had to change my life, for me, and for my family. I had to stop this cycle of self-destruction and pain. That was the gift Dad left me. I became aware of my spiritual journey to see how I was creating my life.

Through meditation, prayer, and writing my thoughts and feelings in a journal, I opened my heart to my truth. It was extremely hard at first. But gradually, I discovered that I am worthy, I am powerful, and most important, I am lovable. I discovered that I am a creative being full of God's light. No longer do I have to go looking on the outside for love. All along it's been on the inside.

Trust is what led me to writing this book. People have been telling me for years to write. I never believed I could. Then messages, through my meditations, were sent my way letting me know what to write. This is where the trust came in. If I had not taken the tiny steps toward faith in God and myself, and learned to trust the messages, then this book wouldn't exist.

Right before this book poured from my soul, I was presented with a miraculous gift. I had gone to the beach to write a letter to a friend with whom I was struggling. I wrote the word "Dear," but instead of my friend's name, I wrote my own. I felt as if a power had taken me over. This is the message that flowed from my pen.

Dear Terri,

I'm writing this letter to share my feelings about our relationship. I love you. You are so special. You have such passion for life and you are so creative. Your mind is amazing. You are able to see things from many perspectives; you are not one-sided. You see the beauty in life and the colors of it.

You are the yin and the yang. There is so much light in you. You shine even in the night. And even when you feel your darkest, you look for the light. That is loving you. Now it's time to forgive. Forgive yourself for what you see as sins. Yes, you can still be judgmental at times. Don't worry…this, too, will end. This has been your greatest teacher. What you have hated, you have now begun to love. Congratulations! You are a light full of God's grace. Be kind to yourself. Be patient.

As for understanding your children, you still have much to learn. This is good. Be aware. Fill them with kindness and care. See them as you and how you separated yourself from love. Don't judge. Love them, as you wanted to be loved. That's all they want, just as you did. You ask, "How do I do that?" Ask "What would Jesus do?" He would forgive and see past their resistance to their pain.

This is what you have to do for yourself. There is still fear inside of you…fear of not being loved and not acknowledged…fear of being controlled. Be aware of these fears. They are your teachers, too. This is how difficult situations are so beneficial to you. Once you can pass through these fears…yes, the time is near…you will feel at once a whole.

Be patient. That is the key. Let divine wisdom saturate your body. You keep it in your mind. Now let it flow through to your heart. "How?" you ask. Follow me. I am here for you. Place your hand in mine and you will fly. Take this time to heal. It is essential. Be at peace, for I am with you always.

Be still,
Me

I don't know how to explain this letter other than to say what my heart feels: I feel as if God sent a message to me. The message is clear. Life is a gift. Every situation we bring into our lives and every fear that we face presents a lesson from which we can learn…each reflecting something that needs to be healed and forgiven in ourselves. I also believe that when you see life as a gift, you sit in gratitude. And when you live a life of gratitude, you live from a space of empowerment, rather than being a victim.

I feel the letter makes reference to Jesus because I see him as a master of truth and forgiveness. He completely lived from his heart and stood up for his beliefs. I feel he embraced all people and exemplified unconditional love. I also believe he was setting an example of how we all can be as children of God. The letter to me poses the question, "What would Jesus do?" This works for me because of what I believe. However, if asking this question doesn't work for you, then ask, "What would love do?" or "What would God do?" What matters here is that you find a connection to the universal truth…God's essence…the love that is inside of you.

The key point of the letter refers to my kids. I feel this is so because my life centers mostly on them. During this last leg of my journey, their approval is what defined me. This is why I struggled with them. I looked for what I thought would make them happy, rather than living from my heart and what I believe. I was also trying to fit into the perfect picture of what society says a good parent should be. Once again, I didn't live authentically.

The letter tells me to see my kids as me and how I separated from love. In this book, I see my children as my teachers. They still are. When I have issues with them, it is because they reflect my pain and fears. Like each of us, I am a child first. When I react to them, it is because I hurt or I'm fearful of what people will think of me. This is not just with my kids, but also with everyone around me.

If you're like most humans, you react to life out of your past experiences. This is the truth whether your life centers on work, family or play. When you react to something or go into blame, it is because you hurt. The little child within is in fear or pain. You have forgotten who you are. Or maybe you never knew your truth in the first place.

I discovered this fact over the last few years. This is why I am sharing my journey with you. I am a spiritual coach. By working with a person's spirit, I feel God uses me to help that person release old fears, negativity and limiting beliefs. This allows the person to live more powerfully in his or her truth. I didn't know I had this gift until after Dad died, when I went within and began to open up to my truth. There was one problem, though: I constantly tried to "fix" myself, rather than accept myself. I didn't realize this until I saw my clients do the same.

My clients were a gift. They reflected my own pain. I began to see them as little children buried beneath societal beliefs, not living from their hearts, but reacting to life from what they felt they should be. I was doing the same.

Then my awareness shifted. I finally remembered the little child within me. A picture of her flashed in my mind during a meditation, and, as I cried and cried, I remembered that she is lovable and acceptable just the way she is. That's where this book begins. I heard a little voice inside of me guide me. It said, "Terri, this is the beginning of your book. Get up and write this." So I did. Through the process of watching my kids and the world around me for almost a year and allowing each situation to reflect my own childhood pain and fears, I got to know that little child within. She is my heart and my soul. And as a result, I discovered who I am and what I believe. And because I gave myself permission to live in my truth, I can now say that I love, accept, and approve of myself. It feels so good! By standing in my truth and sharing it with you, I hope it will give you permission to do the same.

I'm here to tell you that you are an amazing spirit, a child of God. You deserve the love and happiness that you desire. Please don't wait for a catastrophe to happen in your life before you make a commitment to heal.

Healing is a commitment to the self. You create healing by taking tiny steps, one by one, to shift your consciousness. Our society plays to our want of a "quick fix." But true healing doesn't happen that way. If you really want your life to change, then spend this time getting to know yourself.

You are a gift to the world around you. If you don't know this, then you will by the end of this book. You will find the love within by answering the questions and doing the exercises that I have provided for you. They will open up your heart to this truth. As the message sent to me said, the situations you have created in your life are your teachers. It's time to learn from them. It's time to face your fears. It's time to heal the pain. It's time to love you!

Before you get started with your journey, try to find a picture of yourself as a little child, possibly around the age of four or five. Put the picture in a place where you can see it, so that you are reminded to honor and love this child every moment, every day. If you can't find a picture, find something symbolic of your childhood to act as that reminder.

The next step to finding the love within is to create "an intention" to have this in your life. Close your eyes. Picture your life filled with love. Imagine embracing everything about yourself. Imagine letting go of all anger, frustration and blame. Imagine yourself releasing all fear and control. Now keep that picture in your mind and feel the celebration in your body as if you have already reached your goal. Feel it through and through, from the top of your head to the tips of your toes. Then give thanks to God for having helped you create this in your life. By setting this intention, you've taken a giant leap into loving and honoring you and creating the life you've always wanted.

After you have found a picture and set your intention, read my journal. Travel the path with me and let the stories of my life reflect your own pain and fears. Complete the questions after each entry in a journal or notebook of your choosing. The questions will take you deeper within your heart so that you can discover who you are and what you believe, not what you think you are supposed to be to get love and approval. Take some time with this. Allow yourself to heal. Then when your mind is unsettled and confused and you really can't comprehend what is taking place in your life, take this book in hand and ask God what message you need revealed. Either let the book fall open or listen for a page number. You will be astonished at the accuracy of the message given to you.

I believe this book was guided in journal form to be an example for you. Notice in the journal entries how I stay present and focus on each situation that is occurring in my life. It is vital to your growth to be aware, to release all blame, and to stay in the present moment of every situation to receive the gift of healing. Only by living as much in the present as you possibly can will you be able to ask yourself, "Is this what I truly feel and is this what I really want in my life or am I just seeking others' approval?" By asking these questions you release the outside world as the authority of your life and begin to find the love within.

As you make this journey with me, please, be patient with yourself. I've taken out the entry dates of my journal because they have no meaning for you. Please know, however, the entries came very sporadically. The gaps between them were times of integration or times of fear with some of the gaps lasting as long as six weeks. You most likely will experience the same. It's okay…forgive yourself.

Congratulations for taking a giant step into healing your life. Pat yourself on the back for facing your truth. It will be hard at times, and there will be situations you don't want to face. But the love you will find inside and the miracles you will experience as you get into the rhythm and flow of your life are well worth the wait.

The time is here. It's time to open up your heart to the truth. It's time to forgive the pain of the past. It's time to discover the unique, lovable you.

Let the journey begin!

The Journey

REMEMBER THE CHILD WITHIN

Today, I said hello to a little girl. She is sweet and lovable. She is completely acceptable. She is me.

I am mixed with emotions...pain, sadness, joy and happiness...all mixed into one. I realize I forgot her somewhere along the way. I forgot her feelings, her thoughts, her pain. I sit here sobbing for her. I am so joyous for having re-discovered her and so sad for having forgotten her. But she forgives me. She never stopped loving me. That's how children are. . .they instinctively know how to love and forgive. It's just that somewhere along the way, they forget. Children start listening to everyone else's opinions and judgments, and before long, they lose themselves. That's what I did with that little girl inside of me. She got lost along the way, but now I've found her.

"God, help me to love this little child inside of me. Help me to release the guilt I feel for having hurt her. Help me to forgive myself for not having listened to her. Help me to accept myself and to live in my truth. Help me to release the fears that created the separation between her and me and now that which separates me from you. With "you" I mean everything, for I know you are the person on the street, the trees around me, the seagulls on the beach. You are everything and in everything there is love. Please help me to realize that life is a gift. Each moment, each situation, each emotion is a gift of love. Thank you."

Thoughts for Your Journey

It's time to say hello to that little child inside of you. Find a comfortable place to relax. Close your eyes and take a few deep breaths. Let your thoughts flow in and out. Now imagine yourself at a very young age. See that little "you" in front of you. See yourself pulling that child up onto your lap and give him or her a huge embrace. Get to know yourself. You may feel that this is silly. It is okay. Allow yourself to pretend. Have a conversation with this child. Ask what the child feels. Ask for forgiveness for having forgotten him or her along the way. Write what you feel.

We forget the little child inside because we are too busy to listen for what the child needs. To listen, you must clean out your life. It's time to let go of the things that you don't have to do. List five things that are priorities for you and let everything else fall by the wayside. Make sure that at least one of these things is focused on you and only you...not your family or work. It's up to you to make this commitment to healing. You get to choose!

1. Love myself
2. Be playful + laugh again.
3. More patience w/ Bella
4. Support Wade
5. Forgive myself for the past.

FACE YOUR FEARS

I have the cutest little dog. She weighs all of seven pounds. She's a little white ball of fluff. Her name is Squirt and she thinks I'm her mom. Her favorite place to nestle is up on my shoulder. She would lie there forever if I let her.

I took Squirt for a walk today. She is so tiny that she is very afraid of other dogs...especially the BIG ones. Even when she walks by a fire hydrant she runs in the other direction if she smells another dog's scent.

As Squirt and I were walking, I became fearful for her. I became the overprotective mom. I pulled her to the far side when we passed another dog. We came upon a group of men with a big black labrador roaming around without a leash. As Squirt tried to crawl up my leg, I grabbed her up. The owner of the dog watched as we passed in fear. He said, "That dog needs exercise."

With a trembling voice I replied, "I know, but your dog isn't on a leash and it's scaring my dog. We have a leash law around here, you know." Then I proceeded to walk on.

I had to turn back around eventually and knew I was going to have to face this man and his dog again. I decided that I would face my fear this time and let Squirt walk on her own four feet. We passed that big black dog very quietly...it didn't even notice us.

I had a long walk back to my car and a lot of time to think. I saw how when I went into fear, I wanted to control. I wanted that man to do what I thought he should do. Every cell in my body tightened and screamed for him to do things my way...because of my fear. Then I looked at how maybe, just maybe, I had made my dog fearful. Is this possible? I think so.

My dog, just like my kids, echoes my emotions and fears. They all learn from my behavior.

My walk came to an end and there before me stood a little child in a homeless man's body. I ached for him. I saw the pain he must be in, living the life he is leading. He looked so sad and lost. What had happened to him? What fears took over his life? What made him separate from that little boy inside of him?

How about you? What fears separate you from the beautiful little child inside of you? I hear many people say, "I'm not afraid of anything." I don't believe this. If you feel the need to fit it...if you want to always look a certain way...if you judge certain types of people...if you need to always be number one...if you feel you never do things right...if you like everything perfect...if you don't think you're good enough...if you don't think you can speak your feelings...if you eat emotionally. . .and on and on, then you have fear. We all do. It is part of who we are as humans.

What about our spirits? That's who we truly are. We are full of love because we are the essence of God. That is our truth. Now it's time to own it. It's time to speak our feelings and innermost thoughts. It's time to face our fears. It's time to be all we can be. It's inside of us. We don't have to go looking "out there" for love. We don't need other people to fill us up. We don't need anyone to tell us how to be. These things are already inside of us. We just have to trust in the fact that the power is within us. And trusting that you have the power inside of you immediately makes you more powerful.

I realize now that is why I'm here...why we're all here...to remember who we are. We are on this planet to discover the light within each of us. Life is truly a gift, if we choose to see it that way. Just like my walk with my little dog Squirt; I could have chosen to be stuck in blame with the man and his unleashed dog or I could let it go and see the gift of the situation. The gift was that I saw my fear and my reaction to it...separation and control. Then I saw the homeless man and how he seemed separate and fearful. It's all the same. It just comes in different shapes and sizes. It was a moment in my life to experience the darkness so that I could see the light. The light is always there. We just have to look for it.

Thoughts for Your Journey

What are you afraid of? Go back to some of the examples of fears at the end of this entry. See if any of them ring true for you. Write your feelings.

Recall a recent memory when you were in fear. Now close your eyes. Imagine the little child within you and ask what was bothering you. Let all your memories come to mind. Write about this. Ask what was the gift of the situation. Remember, there is something to be learned in every situation. The gift is to recognize what needs to be healed within you.

Start looking for the gifts in all situations. Write five things you are thankful for today.

1. This class
2. The shooting star
3. My faith in God.
4. My family
5. My new life here.

GIVE YOURSELF
PERMISSION TO SPEAK

How can I know how to parent my children when I don't know how to parent myself? How can I love, unconditionally, my kids, or anyone else for that matter, when I have just begun the process to love myself unconditionally?

We use the term "unconditional love" too loosely. Most people seem to think it means that you love someone even when they get into trouble. That is only part of it. I believe to love unconditionally means that you don't try to mold and make people the way you think they should be. It means that you don't interfere with their journeys. You allow them to know their truths without putting your fears and judgments on them. It's agreeing to disagree. It's allowing them and you to be different.

The problem with getting to this step of true unconditional love is that we have to know our own truth first. To be in our own truth means that we live out of love rather than fear, for if you know your own inner truth then you know that it is nothing but love for yourself, and for others. There is nothing that separates you from the world around you. This is my quest in life...to love unconditionally...and my greatest teachers are my kids.

Mackenzie is my first-born daughter and is a mirror to my soul. As I write this, she is eight years old. . .two years older than my younger daughter, Kolbi, and eight years younger than my stepson, A.J.

Mackenzie is the middle child, but because of the age difference between A.J. and her, she is essentially considered a first-born child, just as I am. I have a younger sister, Kelly, on whom I wreaked havoc all through my childhood.

Lately Mackenzie and Kolbi have been fighting like two alley cats. I hear them taunting each other constantly, and they always try to pull me into their battles. I've gotten to the point that I tell them I am not the judge and jury, but now I realize, I have been just that.

Today I picked up Mackenzie from school a little earlier than her sister. She had been on a field trip. As we sat there talking to her very dear friend, we started discussing sibling rivalry. Her friend said, "Mackenzie, I've never seen you being nice to Kolbi." Ouch!

To my horror, Mackenzie said, "I don't care. I don't like her." Then she laughed it off. . .that is until I had to put in my two cents worth.

I proceeded to tell her that her little sister loves her and that she shouldn't feel that way. She said, "Mom, she says the same thing to me."

I really stuck the knife in deep. I responded with "Well, you are the one who started it. She didn't used to be that way."

Mackenzie walked away and wouldn't come near me. In so many words, I had just been the judge and jury and had found her guilty. I watched her from afar as I visited with another mom. We were also sharing the woes of sibling rivalry and how comparisons are deadly, especially when coming from parents. I looked at Mackenzie and realized that once again she was my teacher. It was I who had started this drama with my girls. It's as if they were performing for me to learn about myself. My judgment was forcing Mackenzie to separate from me and to feel very bad about herself.

This is exactly how I used to feel with my sister. I did not like her growing up. I saw her as a conformist who won praise for it, and so, when we were young, I separated from her and my mom. The reality is that I wanted my girls to love each other, just as I know my mom did.

Like so many others, I was trying to make a bad situation better with my words and then only made it worse. I understand that I was putting my old feelings onto my children and not wanting them to feel the same pain as I did. Children are going to fight. I know this. It is a learning ground for future relationships. It's just that when people like me put a judgment on it because of their own past experiences, then it becomes a bad thing.

Mackenzie and I walked to the car. Kolbi had been asked to go to a friend's house. I knew I had to say something to ease the pain I had caused Mackenzie. We sat in the car for a moment very quietly. I said to her, "Mackenzie, I am so sorry for what I said to you."

She burst into tears and replied, "Mom, you made me feel like I am this bad person and that I am to blame for everything!"

I said, "I know, and it's not true. If anyone is to blame, I am. It is natural for sisters to fight. It is even okay for you to not like your sister. I'm the one who has made you feel bad by saying the things I've said. You and your sister are not to blame. Neither one of you is bad. You are both beautiful little beings and are perfect just the way God made you. Mackenzie, I hope you can forgive me. I know God forgives me and now I have to forgive myself." And with that we drove off.

Kids do have a right to feel what is inside of them. . .just as the little kids inside of you and me do. And yet, so much of our society says that we have to conform to be accepted. It is okay to speak your mind. This is not a bad thing. Our judgment on speaking up is what makes us feel bad.

"I have a right to my opinion and then we can discuss it." That is what my mom tells me I proclaimed when I was all of seven years old. But because of the fact that our society says we must hold our feelings inside, I began to feel like a bad person whenever I expressed mine. And, let me tell you, that was often, because I have never been able to keep my mouth shut. Over time, especially during high school, I developed a nasty little chip on my shoulder. I was sure everyone was calling me names behind my back. I didn't feel I had permission to speak out, but since I couldn't help myself, I was sure they were judging me for my "mouthiness."

As Miss U.S.A., when I was twenty, some of my pain melted away. That's because gratitude finally entered my life. When I traveled to other countries and saw the poverty there, I moved into an awareness that my life had been pretty good. On the other hand, the edge was still there. I will never forget when the president of Miss Universe, Incorporated told me I needed to change my looks. I needed to be more glamorous. My response was this, "I got here by being me, so don't even attempt to change me." This did not go over very well. From that point on, I was on that man's black list.

As I moved my way into my mid-twenties and early thirties, I decided I was taking out a new lease on life. I was going to be nice and not so mouthy. Now ironically, when I look back, there were very few people who didn't think I was somewhat nice. They thought I could be a little hot headed, but still nice. I'm the one who painted my picture to be the bad guy. I chose that role. Now I was going to be the really nice guy. Wrong choice! I started holding things in and not speaking my truth to the point that I got pains in my body and even got explosive with my kids at times. Luckily, I didn't hit them, but boy, there were days that I wanted to.

Now, I recognize how my body reacts when I am still working in those old pictures of not being able to express myself. I feel as if I am choking. Then I bring myself into the present moment and tell myself that it is okay for me to speak my truth. When I allow myself to do this, I don't feel the need to be forceful with my opinions. I can state them without feeling apologetic and I don't have to get defensive.

I have a friend, I'll call her Lisa, who is also a great teacher for me. We mirror each other in so many ways. When I find fault with her, when I want to give her all of the blame, I now try to take my judgment from her and look inside myself to see what is hurting. It is never about the other person when we have issues. People around us are the mirrors to our souls, reflections, just as Mackenzie and Lisa are for me.

We recently spent New Year's with some friends, and Lisa's family was there. We found ourselves in a heavy discussion and before I knew it I felt like I was going head to head with her. We often have very different opinions about life. Well, instead of allowing her to speak her mind and being okay with that, I had to jump right in there and speak mine. I saw her as very judgmental and forceful and I didn't like it. It was offending some of my friends. My stomach felt as if it were going to erupt. I pulled myself away from the situation and gave myself a good talking to.

"Now, Terri, you know your truth. It is okay for you to speak it and it is okay for Lisa to speak hers. Why do you have to go to battle over it?" I couldn't get the answer right there. To be honest, I was still reeling over the whole situation.

Once the evening was over and the New Year had begun, I asked God for guidance. I knew there was a gift in this situation; I was just having a hard time seeing it. The answer I received was this.

"Terri, both you and Lisa have very strong opinions about life and that is okay. However, the two of you are still working out of childhood programming that says you can't speak your mind. And, as a result, Lisa and you come off as being very forceful with your words. You speak with force because there is a battle going on within you. Your spirit wants you to speak your truth, but the little child inside of you doesn't feel it can. You must give this child inside of you permission to speak up. If both you and Lisa did this, there would be no reason to be forceful."

When I look back on that night with Lisa and so many other times just like it, I know we were both not being adults in those moments, but rather we were being frightened little children afraid that we would get into trouble for saying what we felt. . .we were afraid to be in our truths. But now I know that is the only way for me to be. I have to be in my truth so that I can love myself, and others, unconditionally.

Thoughts for Your Journey

Do you speak your truth? What thoughts come up for you after reading this entry? Why do you feel you hold your voice inside?

Sit quietly. Ask yourself to recall a time when you were angry with someone for not allowing you to speak. Let the pictures move in and out of your mind. Feel the pain. Let the emotions well up inside. See your inner child and give this child permission to speak from now on.

STOP DENYING YOUR NEEDS

As I heal my life, those around me heal. I am so excited to say that I have seen a huge shift with my girls. They are actually doing things for each other and being nice to one another. The fighting has settled down to a dull roar. They both seem to be feeling a lot better about life since they no longer see themselves as bad.

Ironically, I have been the bear. Frustration has consumed me lately because I see the changes they are making and, yet, I still find myself less than tolerant. I've wanted to run away at times. The only thing that has kept me going is my faith that everything is a gift and that if I pull myself up from the deep water for a moment and ask for guidance, I might be able to see the light. That's what I did last night. I prayed for guidance. I did not get my answer immediately, though. I put the girls to bed and then proceeded to come downstairs to visit with my husband, Steve. Instead, I fell into his arms, sobbing.

"I don't know what it is, but these kids are really getting to me. They are wonderful. It's not them, it's me," I cried to Steve.

As Steve and I talked, the gift was shown to me. One of the big things I struggle with in life is either giving too much or not enough. At this time I had been giving too much and was doing nothing for me. My writing had pretty much come to a standstill and I felt stuck. I have this little metaphor that I use with people all the time. Now it was time for me to heed my own advice. This is it.

Imagine yourself as a cup. If that cup is empty
and yet you still give and give to everyone around you

and don't fill that cup up by giving to yourself, then that cup begins to get brittle and cracks into many little pieces. It gets angry and resentful. Before long that cup doesn't exist anymore. You lose yourself.

On the other hand, if you see yourself as a cup and you fill it with love for yourself and give to yourself some of the things you need, then that cup becomes so full that eventually it overflows to others all around it. Your life becomes abundant and full of love. As a result, the love touches everyone.

It's truly amazing how life works. Life can feel as if it is in chaos. It can make you feel you want to run away. But if you open your eyes to what's occurring in your life and ask for the gift, it will be revealed. In this instance, life was telling me that the little girl inside of me needed to be taken care of, too. It was telling me that her feelings needed to be acknowledged. I resented my kids and felt angry and hurtful because I wasn't honoring my needs.

Before we can see, hear and feel others' needs, we must acknowledge our own first. This sounds selfish. It is not. Society tells us to put others first and to forget our own needs. But this isn't working. Anger, frustration, and hate torment our world because people do not feel loved. That's because most people are looking for love from the outside world, rather than filling up their own cups. I can only imagine what this world would be like if we each took responsibility for ourselves and filled up our own cups. If we nurtured and loved ourselves, our cups would fill up and the love would overflow to the world around us.

Thoughts for Your Journey

Is your cup empty or full, or somewhere in between? What are you personally lacking in your life right now?

What's holding you back from having a full cup? Talk to that little child inside of you again and ask what needs to be forgiven within you so that you will allow yourself abundance in your life.

The quickest way to manifesting anything in your life is to give thanks to God for already having received it.

I'm still lacking total freedom from my Dickey days. But I'm making great progress and I'm relieved to be able to let this go & understand.

THE GIFT OF MEDITATION

Do you ever allow yourself to be completely in the present moment? This may sound like a silly question, but how often do you sit quietly and just "be?" Allowing yourself to absorb the present time is like a "Kodak moment." The colors are brilliant and you notice things you've never noticed before. It's like looking at a picture for the first time and being inspired by its pure beauty. I had a moment like that today.

I was at my girls' elementary school, working as a parent volunteer in Kolbi's first grade class. It was lunchtime and she had convinced me to "hang out" for a while. I visited with her and some friends and then found myself looking around at all of the kids. Life stood still. I watched the kids standing in the lunch line, but what I really saw were a bunch of beautiful little beings. They were so full of eagerness to learn and play and explore. Their eyes, arms and hearts were open to the world. They were love in the purest sense.

This moment was such a gift. I felt as if I were seeing the human race for the first time. This is how being in the present moment works. It allows you to feel alive. . .to be connected to the world around you. . .to let go of all your worries and guilt. It allows you to see the gifts of life.

One of the ways I've slowed down enough to be in the present moment is through meditation. People often ask me how I do that. There is no right or wrong way. You just sit quietly and "be."

I would like to share a simple meditation with you. This meditation centers you and helps you to be fully present.

Find a relaxed position. Close your eyes. Take several deep breaths. Tighten everything on your body,

 *Message Sent* 43

as tight as you can, and then relax. Let your body sink deeper. Give thanks to God for the healing you are about to receive.

Now imagine a beautiful golden light coming down from God and connecting to the crown of your head. Feel the warmth of this light. Let the light continue down through your face and neck, relaxing your forehead and throat. Allow it to pour into your arms, flooding out the palms of your hands and fingertips. Put no effort into this. Just allow it to happen.

This beautiful iridescent light pours into your chest region, opening up your heart to God's love. It continues flowing down around your rib cage, through your power region, releasing all of your fears.

Allow the light to relax your stomach and lower back, releasing all of your emotional tension. Then send it down to the root of your torso, allowing your survival fears to be released.

Now imagine a huge tube of light. Visualize it from the bottom of your torso, expanding down around your legs and continuing down to the center of the earth. Continue to send the light down this tube and down your legs. Let that light flow out from the balls of your feet and toes.

Envision all of the negativity and fear releasing from your body and being sent down that tube of light to the center of the earth. This completely grounds you and brings you into the present moment.

This is just one form of meditation. Again, there is no right or wrong way. You have to find what feels good for you.

After allowing this light to fill me up, I ask, "God, what is it that you want me to know today?" Then I sit quietly.

Sometimes the answers come from pictures in my mind that show me what I need to know, and then there are other times where I just have to sit and listen.

Listening can be really hard for some, and it has often been very difficult for me. I like to fix things and have a tendency to want to control and do things my way. So, to just listen can be quite a chore for me. This is okay if you have the same problem, too. Allow the thoughts to flow until you relax again. This takes a little practice. You can start out doing this for five minutes a day and work up to what is a comfortable place for you.

It is so important to create this space for yourself. When you can go within to find your answers, then there is no reason to go looking for them on the outside. This is especially beneficial when looking at what is your truth.

A great gift was presented to me some time ago. . .that's when I really began to go within to find my truth. Renee, who didn't know me well then, but who now is one of my dearest friends, told me that she had heard I didn't spend enough time with my kids. She said a friend of hers told her I was never at home. Well, if you want to rock a mom's world, tell her what she's doing wrong. I was shaking all over. At first I started to question her as to why she would say something like that and where she got her information. But then I caught myself. I knew there had to be a gift here. I got in my car and drove away. I pulled into a shopping center parking lot and began to meditate.

"Dear God," I said, "I know there is a message here for me. Please let me hear it, because this really hurts."

This was the answer I heard. "Terri, judgment surrounds everything and you will continue to hear it. What you have to do now is ask yourself what is your truth. That is all that matters."

I asked myself, "What is my truth?"

The answer I received was this. "Terri, you are a great mom. One of the main reasons you began your spiritual journey was so that your children would have a loving atmosphere to live in. Part of creating a loving atmosphere is for you to have time for yourself, and with your husband."

I knew this was true and I also knew immediately who had made the remarks to Renee about me not spending enough time with my kids. This lady's child always spent the night on Steve's and my date night. Because I now knew my truth from meditating on it and felt no more anger or hurt, I was able to look at this woman with great compassion. I knew she didn't allow herself enough time with her husband or alone and that she didn't know how to create it for herself, so she found fault with me. I was able to love my truth and myself and, as a result, was able to love her and understand her pain.

This is what meditation can do for you. It lets you find a space to be in the present moment. It is a tool for releasing the past and the future, allowing you to be in the "now." Being in the "now" creates a bond with everything around you. It slows you down enough to go within to find your own answers. And it helps you to create an existence where you can be child-like in the moment, experiencing all the wonders and the gifts of life.

Thoughts for Your Journey

Try the meditation. What comes up for you? If you have a question, your answer may come to you right now. On the other hand, stay aware and be in the present moment as much as you can today. Your answer may come through a song on the radio, a newspaper ad, or through a conversation with a friend. Stay in the moment and you will eventually get an answer. Write about your experience.

Sit by yourself quietly today, outside, if you can. This can even be on your lunch hour. Take some deep breaths and bring yourself into the "now." Watch the world around you. Write your discoveries.

BE THE ARTIST OF YOUR LIFE

Imagine life as a big play and each and every person is an actor under contract to play his or her part. Now playing a part does not mean that the person has to be charming, handsome, or successful. Playing a part might mean that the actor is playing a bum, a drug addict or a killer. It means that the actor encompasses all the aspects of that character, both good and bad.

Now imagine that all of the people in your life are part of a play. You have a spiritual agreement with one another to create instances and situations to help you remember your spirit…that's if you choose to remember.

The benefit of looking at life this way is that you can start taking responsibility for your part in the play. I believe that we are each spirits who are the purest essence of God. I believe we make agreements to come into this life to help one another remember who we really are.

I see each of us as this loving spirit that enters into life through a baby's body. I see that baby as a beautiful canvas. The canvas is perfect in its own sense. It has a certain grain and texture that make it unique unto itself. The blank canvas is pure perfection because it is just the way it is supposed to be.

Now visualize all of the people who come into that baby's life as "artists." They want to create what they think is a masterpiece. They add a little color here and there. Before long, the colors start getting muddied and you can no longer see that perfect little being. Over time, that beautiful little child will be lost, never having any idea that it was perfect to begin with.

I believe this is our agreement…that we each come in with our own uniqueness, much like the grain and texture of the canvas. But because we are surrounded with people who don't know their truths and are not coming from that pure sense of oneness and love, judgment surrounds us. And because of this, conditioning and programming from our parents, teachers and society are projected onto us. As children, we take them on and make them our so-called truths. But because the information is not our truth, since we are all unique, we become lost…we become fearful…we become separate from the world around us.

This feeling of separateness is what made me want to control the world around me. I thought by controlling things that I could make people love me. I also thought that by controlling my stepson, and eventually my girls, and making them act a certain way that this would bring love to them from the outside world. This is what we do as a society. We put our beliefs on our children as to what we think will bring them love and acceptance. Parents do it, as well as teachers. This programming sticks with us for the rest of our lives causing us to react to life with pain and negativity.

"Mommy, I keep trying my best and my teacher still yells at me." Kolbi sobbed those words every day for the first week of school this year. This broke my heart and made me want to yank her out of the classroom, but instead I went within and asked what I should do.

This teacher reminds me of my first grade teacher who was quite controlling and taught through fear. I do have to say, however, that Kolbi's teacher is considered a great teacher, but is very strict and very stern. Kolbi sees the teacher's sternness as yelling. When I meditated on this situation, I got an answer that surprised me. I was told that Kolbi had created this situation to connect to her truth. Well, I kept forgetting that. Every time I walked into that classroom I wanted to take her teacher and tell her what I thought of her. That was the little girl inside of me reacting to the pain of the past.

Then one day, the truth hit me. This was the perfect opportunity to let Kolbi see the gift of the situation. Kolbi constantly says her teacher expects everything to be perfect. When I finally saw the light, I was able to explain to Kolbi that her teacher is a great gift and that if there is something she doesn't like about her, then she doesn't have to accept the teacher's truth for herself. I expressed to Kolbi that just because the teacher seems to feel that perfection is needed, that doesn't mean Kolbi has to be that way. I did tell her that, while she needs to follow a teacher's rules in the classroom, she doesn't have to "own" them for her truth. I told her she should go inside her heart to find out who she is, not by what someone tells her how to be. I have to say I was so proud of myself. Now the big question was how to exercise the same information for myself. I had to go within to find my truth.

I finally discovered the gift for me in this situation when I saw that I was trying to control Kolbi's teacher! Of course, what I was finding wrong with her was what I found inside of me. I was in fear. I was being controlling. I felt so controlled by my first grade teacher and because I didn't have tools to understand that this was my teacher's information, I took it on as my own. I was afraid that Kolbi would do the same because of her teacher. It was my fear of wanting to protect her from this situation that made me want to control her teacher. I know now that I don't have to feel this fear, because I've given Kolbi tools to help her find her own truth. Now it's up to her to choose. She can be a victim or she can be empowered by using the tools.

I believe that Kolbi, her teacher, and I were in a spiritual agreement to learn about ourselves. I see how I reacted to Kolbi's teacher out of my own past childhood programming from my first grade teacher. And Kolbi learned how to find her truth without ever taking on her teacher's programming. I also see how I wanted to control Kolbi's teacher and how her being controlling was a reflection to me. I still have moments of wanting to control Kolbi's teacher, but now I can find some gratitude for the gift she is revealing.

When we know that we are co-creating our world around us so that we can reconnect to our spirits and we take responsibility for that, then we can change our view of the world. When we realize that everything we need is inside of us and it's just the muddied paint that keeps us from seeing it, then we can remember who we truly are.

I am so thankful that I didn't yank Kolbi out of that classroom. It has been such a gift and an awakening. Kolbi and I are both becoming the artists of our lives, releasing the societal programming that muddies our unique canvases.

Thoughts for Your Journey

How is societal programming affecting your life? In what areas of your life are you trying to meet someone else's expectations? In what ways are you putting your own programming and conditioning onto other people?

Think of a situation that causes you great frustration due to expectations. Take two pieces of white paper. On one, color how you feel about this situation when you are doing what feels right in your heart. On the other piece of paper, color how you feel when you are trying to live outside your truth by meeting expectations. Write down your discoveries. Forgive yourself for having stayed in the picture that is not you.

ACCEPT YOUR HUMANNESS

I find it ironic that I am able to share my journey with you in this book. After my dad died, I tried to write in a journal. I found it very difficult to do. Months would pass by without writing a word. In my mind, that amount of writing wasn't good enough. I felt extremely frustrated because I couldn't put my thoughts and feelings on paper the way I felt they should be written. I had too many expectations.

My whole life has been filled with expectations. There have been so many times that I felt as if my life were hopeless. I felt that I would never be truly happy. I'm sure some people around me thought I was being ungrateful for what I had in life. In some ways they were probably right. My lifestyle has always been one of "havingness" and I have never really wanted for anything. . .except to feel loved. The problem was that I wanted everyone else to give me that feeling.

Expectations can destroy relationships. I used to put a lot of expectations on my husband. If he did things just the way I asked him, then I thought that meant he loved me. At least I felt that way for a moment or two. The feeling usually wore off pretty quickly, especially when I created another expectation for him to fulfill. The expectations were never-ending. If he didn't fulfill my expectations, then boy, was he dirt. And on top of it all, I felt horrible, too, because I still didn't feel truly loved. Love doesn't come from the outside. It comes from within you.

If I put one expectation on others, then I put a thousand on myself. In my mind I could never do anything right or good enough. This would cause great anger and frustration in my life. Most of the time it was vented towards others. I never knew that I was really mad at myself. I just knew I had a raging anger and constantly felt like a volcano waiting to erupt. Then to add fuel to the fire, I would get angrier with myself for having gotten angry in the first place. If this sounds a little confusing, that's exactly how I felt inside: confused!

Then one day further into my journey, I had an epiphany. To be angry for feeling anger is crazy. Of course I have the right to feel anger. It is a natural emotion. Anger can let you know when something is not right in your world. It's a red flag to tell you to look around and see what's going on in your life. Anger became a burden because I put a judgment on it that it was a bad thing.

"Terri, you have a very bad temper just like me. You need to learn to start holding it in a little better." My dad said this to me when I was a teenager.

Yikes! What I really needed was the freedom to express my anger in a safe setting. But this was my dad's opinion because he never learned how to express his anger. He felt it was "expected" of him to suppress his anger. He expected the same from me. I don't blame him. I realize now it was the only way he knew to help himself. I feel that it was this withholding of expression that eventually led to his death. He bottled up so much of his pain and anger that it stayed in his body until he became sick at the very young age of 54. And that's exactly what I began to do. Pain and sickness invaded my body because of withholding my feelings. There was "dis-ease" in my body; therefore, there was disease. I believe that is how disease begins. I believe it starts with suppressed pain and suffering, otherwise known as "dis-ease."

Pain and suffering were tremendous catalysts for the decision to heal my life. I did not want to be angry anymore and I definitely did not want to be sick. I wanted peace. I wanted to be whole and I wanted my family to feel whole. I've finally begun to find this for myself and as a result, my family is healing, too. I am being the example for them. But as I said earlier, it has taken great persistence. There were days when I was blinded by anger and frustration, usually due to having too many expectations. I had to forgive myself for this. Then I had to find a way to let the anger out. That's when I began writing a journal. Only some days I felt so much emotion that I wanted to ram a pencil into a wall rather than write with it. I had to discover a way to vent my rage physically, yet in a safe way. My bed became my punching bag. I took a pillow many times and beat the heck out of it. I still do this on those occasions when I get overwhelmed with life. This tool can work for people of all ages.

Kolbi came home from school the other day after having a rough day. She said, "Mom, I feel so angry I think I could kick a hole in the car!"

I told Kolbi that it was okay to feel anger and that it is a natural emotion. However, I told her that I thought a better way to handle it would be to smack the bed with a pillow. She thought this was quite funny. So we proceeded to take pillows in hand and beat the daylights out of my bed. Kolbi got out her frustrations and we ended up having a fun pillow fight and tickle fest.

Another trick I like is to scream at the top of my lungs. I especially like doing this in my car. It feels so good to get the anger out. Exercise is another way that releases tension for me. Dance is another. I'll turn on some music very loudly. . .I love hip-hop. . .and dance and bounce around until I feel like I've shaken all of the stress out of me.

I have found that, once I let some of the anger and frustration out, I can be still and calm enough to ask for guidance and listen for the answer. This calmness also affords me the ability to write about what's going on inside. Sometimes just allowing myself to express freely is all I need.

Expressing your emotions is one of the greatest gifts you will ever give to yourself. As you start letting some of the anger and disappointment out and begin to find forgiveness for yourself for having held onto it in the first place, before long there's very little anger left. When you finally let go of some of the expectations in your life, you start experiencing the love that is inside of you, the love that has always been there. Giving yourself permission to be human is the key.

Thoughts for Your Journey

Go into awareness of when you are putting expectations on yourself and others. When you see yourself in this kind of situation, notice how you are feeling. What happens to your body? Get to know your body language when you are in emotional pain. Write about your discoveries with this.

What would you say if you could express yourself freely right now? Are you filled with anger or sadness? Allow the pain to come out. If you feel as if it is there but won't come to the surface, then just "be" with this. Go into awareness and see when you repress your feelings and thoughts with other people. Give yourself permission to be human and feel.

TAKE AWAY ALL BLAME

Like a caterpillar becoming a butterfly, I've withdrawn from the real world for a while. I had to go within to find out how to fly. I withdrew from life, as I knew it, and that meant withdrawing from people and things around me. When you decide to change your life, everything changes.

You see, as your journey begins, there tends to be a lot of resistance to the change. People are set in their ways and want things to stay familiar. So as you begin to change and "own" your power, they don't quite know what to do with it. You may find yourself now butting heads and blaming people you used to agree with on everything. Your family might tell you you're wrong and you might find your friends falling by the wayside. Remember, this has been your choice. I had to remember that yesterday.

My friend called me out of the blue and asked me to go with her to a concert. I was very excited that she had thought of me. Lately I've really been ready to get back into my social life since I've found some inner peace. Well, that inner peace was blown right out of the window when she told me who had already turned down her invitation. The little girl inside of me quickly added two and two together and realized that she wasn't at the top of her friend's list. Ouch! I immediately felt separate from her and blamed her for my pain. But knowing that there is always a gift of love in every situation, I let go of the blame and began to heal the pain.

For the rest of the day I flashed back on my childhood and remembered similar situations. For instance, the time I called my friend in the third grade to see if she could play. She said her mom said she couldn't. Well, lo and behold, when I showed up at another friend's house a little while later to see if she could play, the friend who had turned me down was there.

Those memories are painful and we all have them. And yet, we tend to suppress the pain and try to forget. The problem is that the brain doesn't forget. Negative charges are stored in the brain. Then as time goes by, we tend to forget the initial circumstance that caused the pain in the first place. As we grow older, we still react out of those negative charges and most of the time we don't know why. As a result, we tend to blame others for our pain. That is why it is so important for us to get to know ourselves. If, for instance, you are constantly finding fault with your spouse, your children, your friends or a boss, ask yourself what it "lights up" for you. In other words, what memories and emotions arise for you? The answer will most likely go back to your childhood.

Kolbi came home the other day and was very blue because a boy had been mean to her. She blamed him for hurting her feelings. I've taught my kids a meditation to be done in an imaginary garden. In this garden they sit on a bench. They can ask their guardian angels to come to talk to them, they can talk to God, or they can ask someone they have an issue with to appear. In this case, I told Kolbi that maybe she should go into the garden and ask the little boy's spirit to come forward and ask him why he was being mean to her.

"Mom, he says he is being mean to me because his mom and dad are mean to him. He says he doesn't feel anyone is nice to him."

In that moment, with what could have been a charge that affected Kolbi negatively for a lifetime, she found compassion. That charge could have caused her great pain like the ones I had from my own childhood dramas. Instead, by going into her garden and finding her truth, the blame was released and compassion was found. Kolbi discovered the judgment she felt from the little boy was not really about her, but about his own pain.

This meditation can work for you, too. To let the pain of the past become just that, the pain of the past and not the present, we have to get to know ourselves. We have to dig deep within and find out who we truly are. We must have compassion for ourselves. And we have to communicate.

We must first communicate with ourselves and then with the people we still blame. This doesn't have to be communication just with people now, but it can also be with people from the past. We can go to that garden and ask them what the gift was for us to see in a particular situation with them. We can first vent our anger with them, if need be, and then take away the blame and begin to communicate.

We don't tend to have introspective conversations as children and so we build our lives on misperceptions. But when you can go to that garden and ask for the truth, the truth sets you free. No longer will you have to react to things and not know why. No longer will you have to blame your spouse for thinking he or she is trying to control you, when all along it was your charge of being controlled by your mother or father. And no longer will you have to feel as if you are not doing a good enough job with your work because you have been reacting out of an old childhood charge where you felt a teacher said you weren't good enough. And finally, no longer will you have to feel as if you are not likeable and can't have solid friendships, because of past childhood hurts. These are all examples of how those negative charges can affect us in our daily lives. It's time to start letting them go.

If you have trouble communicating with a person during your meditation because you can't get by your negative emotions, then try to see the other person as a child. Ask that child what is hurting in his or her life. You will be amazed at how much compassion comes when you are looking into the eyes of a child. And whatever you do, don't forget to talk to the little child within you and have compassion for him or her, too.

The main thing to remember as you make your journey to the butterfly stage is that it is imperative to communicate with yourself and, if need be, with others, both from the present and the past and to release all blame. You have to ask yourself what is hurting inside to know who you truly are. It is a process that can take a long time. And often when you think you are absolutely ready to take flight as that butterfly, you find yourself hit in the face with more old pictures…just as I did when my friend called…and you want to slide right back into the cocoon. It's okay. Give yourself a break and pat yourself on the back for recognizing the areas that need healing. What matters here is that you are taking the time to honor and love you. And by honoring and loving yourself, then it becomes easier for you to honor and love life.

Thoughts for Your Journey

What pictures pop up in your mind and what feelings surface after reading this? Is there someone you blame in your life? Write your feelings towards this person.

Imagine yourself in a beautiful garden. See it any way you choose. Now visualize a bench where you can take a rest. Take some deep breaths. Allow yourself to relax in this space. Picture the person you blame sitting down with you. Express yourself and allow that person to do the same. Now release the blame. If you have trouble with this, try to see the other person as a child and ask what pain he or she is reacting to when having conflict with you. Ask what this is reflecting for you. Write your discoveries.

LOVE WHAT YOU HATE

Life is a series of opportunities to discover who you are and what you believe so that you may create a life of love, truth, and authenticity. Some of those opportunities can seem a little harsh. But when you make your way through them they can be the greatest gifts of your life. Today I recognized one of those gifts.

My girlfriend, Renee, and I see eye-to-eye on many things. We recognize the roles we play in each other's lives and how we learn from each other. In the process we are both finding our truths. I know I am a person who tends to be resistant in the face of change or in the face of something that is not in my belief system. I need to experience things to believe them. That's who I am, and I am finally learning to accept it.

Renee had a beautiful spiritual experience recently and as a result, she is very passionate about it. She wants everyone to have the same experience. Because I did not have the same experience, I don't have the same passion for it. I felt she was judging me because I didn't buy all of her viewpoints. As a result, I became more resistant to her and she became, what I felt to be, more controlling. A wedge was being driven between us. That is, until today.

Today, I realized how resistance is a great teacher for me. As I felt she was trying to control me, it forced me to go within and find my truth. In that moment I felt overwhelming love for her. I saw her as this beautiful spirit who loved me and was helping me find what was right for me. The irony is that in the moment of my realization, the resistance lifted. Love what you hate. I hear that so often, but in that moment I felt as if her controlling me was something I hated. As soon as I recognized what I was learning from the situation, the love came.

Thoughts for Your Journey

Is there resistance in your life, either by someone being resistant to you or you being resistant to that person? Or are you being resistant to a situation in your life? How does it make you feel?

Now close your eyes and go into your meditation garden, or take some time to write in a journal, or do whatever you choose to communicate with yourself. Then ask what you can learn from this resistance. Remember to take the blame away, both from others and from yourself. This is how you get the answers that truly heal your life. What do you discover?

IN THE DARKNESS
ARE MANY POSSIBILITIES

"Dear God, what are you trying to tell me about my life? Everything is so dark right now. Please, God, show me the gift. I need to see the light."

My mother had a stroke yesterday. I am on my way to Arkansas. I pray that God will heal her pain.

I know there is a message for me, too. Within a ten-minute period yesterday, I felt my world come falling at my feet. It began when I received a call from a woman who recently asked me to go to work in her healing center. She is the one who pursued me. Now she's given me a kick out the door and I haven't even begun to work for her. She told me she doesn't want "another Indian chief in the mix."

And now this. Within moments of getting the boot, I received the telephone call from back home. The lady on the phone introduced herself and explained to me that Mom had been admitted to the hospital earlier that morning due to a stroke. I felt like I was drowning.

So now, as the engines roar and I settle in for the long ride back home, I have to remind myself that in the darkness there are many possibilities. It doesn't feel as if it could get much darker right now. I just have to keep the faith. . .I have to believe that somewhere in here is a gift for both my mom and me to take.

Thoughts for Your Journey

What is bringing darkness to your life right now? Become aware of how your body is responding. See when you are in fear. Write about your discoveries over the next few days.

Recite the affirmation, "In the darkness, there are many possibilities." Try to let go of your resistance to the darkness. Remember, "what you resist will persist." The more you allow yourself to be in the darkness and accept it, the sooner the darkness will go away. Give thanks to God for revealing the gift of this situation. Write about your experience.

Stop the Drama

Dungeons and Dragons is a game kids play, but it's also an appropriate description of my brain.

My brain holds me captive. It keeps me in fear. It keeps me holding the reins of my life pulled in tight. I have created mental dramas my whole life. These dramas kept me chained to the darkest recesses of my mind. I was reminded of this today.

I met a man while at breakfast with my mother's fiancè. Mom is still in the hospital recovering from her stroke. This man used to work with a top government agency. He almost scared the holy daylights out of me with his fearful stories about what's going on in the background of our lives. That's because he was in fear. You could hear it in his voice. You could feel the control of his words. He wanted us to buy into his very fearful drama.

Well, I almost did. But then I started to subtly disagree with him. There was no way I was going to get caught up in his drama. I didn't need this kind of fear. I do a good enough job creating my own.

And that's why he was a gift to me. I asked God why this man had come into my life at this moment. The answer was so that I could see a mirror, a picture of me.

I understand, finally, how I must look to other people. I see I must push my fear on them. I have wanted so badly for the people around me to heal, especially my mom. Over the last few days I have had plenty of one-on-one conversations with our family members. I kept trying to explain to them how important it is for Mom to let go and heal her childhood pain. Well, you can only imagine how they must have felt. By me sounding off out of fear, I reminded them of their own painful pasts. My relatives didn't ask for this. I just shoveled it on them. Every time I brought up this topic, each family member's face turned a nice shade of red. You could tell I had crossed the line with each of them.

So now, as I look at this, I know that I was creating my own little drama. Obviously, I don't want to lose my mom. I have been in great fear about this. The ironic thing is that she is doing great! I am the one who is holding on to the pain. Out of this fear I got stuck wanting to control everything and everyone around me. I got stuck in the recesses of my mind. . .in the dungeon. And the dragons, my fears, have been eating away at me. This was my story, much like the man's story. I was so scared that I tried to control my family and drag them into my drama.

My friend, Renee, likes to call these dramas our movies. We create them in those dark recesses of our minds. And when our movie isn't dramatic enough, we often get involved with others' movies. Just like I almost did with the government man at breakfast. I came very close to getting caught up in his fear, in his very dramatic movie.

My life has always been full of dramas. I believe that I felt so unfulfilled that I had to create excitement in my life. I needed something to make me feel alive.

I comprehend all of this now. I don't need to create any movies in my life and I definitely don't need to buy into other people's stories. This is why it is so important for me to discover who I am. I have to bring in the light. And the light is through God. I know this more and more each day. This is how I can release the dramas of my life and truly feel alive.

Thoughts for Your Journey

What drama are you involved with right now in your life? These dramas can be something as simple as gossip or buying into someone else's fears that you haven't even looked at for yourself. Try to feel if these fears are true for you. What do you discover about yourself?

Write down ways you can stop the dramas. Become aware of when you are getting caught up in them and when you are stuck in negativity. When you see yourself creating a drama or getting caught up in one ask, "What am I afraid of here?" Get to know what causes you to create this in your life. Do you thrive on drama? Is your life so empty and boring that you have to create some excitement in your life? Are you acting out of fear? What are your thoughts about this?

Try this exercise: Every time you go into fear of anything in your life, visualize yourself handing the reins of your life over to God and allowing trust to take over the fear.

RELEASE THE BOUNDARIES
OF YOUR MIND

The truth has been revealed to me. When I left two weeks ago for Arkansas because of my mother's stroke, I was in a panic and surrounded by darkness. I asked God what it was that I needed to see. Boy, did God show me!

First off, I was shown just how controlling I can be when I am in fear. I wrote recently about the woman at the healing center who had asked me to work for her and then gave me the boot before I ever started. She was right. She didn't need another Indian chief in the mix. I was being a bit controlling with her, because I was in fear. The boundaries of my mind said this was what I had to do to be able to do my work. I wasn't listening to my heart that said I really didn't want to work in a regular job with her. So what did I do? I started controlling her. She was right to give me the boot. What a great gift. I am so thankful she could see the light when I couldn't.

From this experience, I also learned what really matters in life. I was very caught up in being ousted by this lady. It really lit up all of my rejection pictures. Everything was put into perspective when my mom was hospitalized by her stroke.

This brings me to the fear of death. There is nothing I can do to control this. I prayed and prayed for my mom's recovery, but I had to relinquish any controls over her possible death. I had to turn to trust. I had to trust that God's will would be done.

I feel like I have taken a huge jump on my spiritual journey. It is so very true, in the darkness there are many possibilities.

So now I look at all of my possibilities for the future and

I know there are no boundaries. My fears kept the chains intact in the past, but not anymore. God showed me this on my plane ride home from Arkansas.

I needed to escape so I read Danielle Steel's novel, *Bittersweet*. What a gift this was to me. The story centered around a woman bound by the chains of her husband's conventional ways. He didn't want her to work, not even on occasion. She, on the other hand, had great gifts that she needed to express and felt very stifled. A man who believed in her came into her life. He was a friend who had faith that she could live beyond the boundaries and still be a mother and wife. She didn't have to be trapped in her husband's fears.

I knew in the first few pages that this book was meant for me to read. I had actually bought it before the flight going to Arkansas, but never felt like opening it. How appropriate that after all of the revelations of the past two weeks, I would decide to read this now.

Bittersweet was an analogy for me. I saw my brain as the husband. It keeps me in chains, bound by fear. The leading lady who had gifts to express, but didn't know how to break free, was just like me. And the friend who supported her, I found to be just like God's love in my heart. . .listening and full of belief in me.

After much contemplation of this book, and after reflecting on my life, I knew I no longer wanted to be stuck within boundaries. . . in the dungeons of my mind.

I feel such excitement from knowing there are so many possibilities. I don't have to be in fear. I'm making a choice right here, right now. I am asking God to help me live beyond all of the boundaries of my mind. I know this truth can be mine, right now, in this moment in time!

Thoughts for Your Journey

Boundaries such as curfews for kids, standing up for ourselves, and many others are needed in life. On the other hand, there are boundaries that keep us stuck in what we think life ought to be, rather than what would make us happy. What boundaries surround your life that affect you negatively?

If you chose to release some of the confining boundaries in your life, what would it be like? What's holding you back from letting those chains go right now?

RELAX, STOP WORRYING, AND ENJOY THE RHYTHM OF LIFE

Water pours over Kolbi's little fingers. She watches it cascade down onto her hands. She takes the soap from the dispenser and begins to wash her hands with intensity and wonder. She slowly rinses them and then begins to dry each finger, one at a time. She is completely in the moment. She is living in the now.

My first inclination is to tell Kolbi to hurry up and come on. However, when I slow myself down long enough, I see that she has something to teach me. I see the beauty of life in every breath she takes and movement she makes. Luckily, all of my rushing her over the years has not taken away this passion. It's not too late for me to recapture this in my life, too. I've slowed down some over the years, but in watching her, I see there is room for more absorbing life in the moment.

We are on vacation, surrounded by one of the most beautiful and enchanting places I've ever seen. We are in Sedona, Arizona. This oasis in the desert allows me, once again, to see myself through my kids' lives. Each day is an opportunity to look at my life with a microscopic eye.

Kolbi, Mackenzie and I find ourselves on horseback. This is the second day we hit the trails of the Coconino National Forest. Larry, a kind-hearted cowboy, is our guide. Mackenzie can't get her horse to mind, so Larry has her connected to a lead rope. Kolbi follows and I bring up the tail.

I fight my horse due to a sore rump caused by a three-hour ride the day before. I look up in front of me and there is Mackenzie. She is in fear. She doesn't express it, but I can see it is shutting her down. She can't get her horse to do anything because she is afraid of the "what ifs." She's fearful of what might happen if she gets her horse to move. The fear freezes her so much that she needs the lead rope.

I see myself in her and can feel her fear and pain. I see how my whole life I have allowed the "what ifs" to sneak in. Whether it's with my work, my writing, my responsibilities as a mom, or just having fun, I have allowed my mind to take me out of the moment and freeze me in fear of what the future might hold.

I love Mackenzie and I am so thankful for the gift she has just shown me. I also realize that she is making her choices, and that right now she is choosing to be in fear, much as I have done in my life and still at times do. But it is a choice.

Then I glance up at Kolbi. She has become "at one with her horse." She looks like she is connected to it. As we move up and down the mountains, her body sways in motion with the horse.

I recognize what her spirit is showing me. I begin to relax into my saddle. I am astonished to see that as I relax and let go of my fear of hurting, the pain subsides. I become at one with my horse. . .except when we take off galloping. I'm sorry to say, but that's when I have a hard time getting my rump to be at one with anything! I'm sure if I had been at one with my horse on my prior ride, then I wouldn't be hurting now.

Once the galloping subsides, I am able to relax back into the rhythm of the ride. I'm finding that's how life is. Sometimes we go into fear, sometimes we start galloping through life so fast that we lose our stride, and sometimes we just need to seek comfort and hide. Then we stop. We take a breath, get back into stride and, if we allow ourselves, absorb each glorious moment while on the ride.

Thoughts for Your Journey

Do you allow yourself to relax and enjoy life? Or are you in a constant state of worry and fear? How does this journal entry reflect the "what ifs" in your life? Are you afraid to make changes in your life because you are fearful of what the future might hold? What are you afraid of here?

What fear are you willing to face today? This can be something as simple as needing to give yourself some time for exercise or some "down time." Write down your feelings and then act upon them.

Life is How We Choose to See It

Coyotes howl in the distance while two black ravens circle and dance above us. The wind whips and the rain spits, as if to welcome us. All of the elements are here to celebrate our union. Steve and I are getting remarried.

It is our tenth anniversary and my gift to my husband was to ask him to marry me again. Because I recently decided to live beyond the boundaries of my normal life, we are getting remarried on top of a knoll overlooking the majestic red rocks of Sedona. A Navajo named Uquala will guide us through our Native American ceremony.

Our whole visit in Sedona has been special and unique. The weather has been absolutely breathtaking and very warm, until today. When we awoke this morning the temperature had dropped, the winds were howling, and it was raining on and off. I was completely dismayed. How could this be happening on our wedding day? I got so blue that I almost called the whole thing off. Then I got my head back together and said, "So what? Maybe we'll get drenched. I guess this is just the way it is supposed to be. After all, when we had our honeymoon here, it rained the whole time. All we did was sleep."

So I gathered my family together and made our way to the wedding site. When we met Uquala there, we started complaining about the weather. He quickly changed our minds.

"Oh, no," he said, "you are very blessed. All of the spirits are here to celebrate your marriage. The wind, the rain, the sun, the coyotes. . .they are all here to give you their blessings. The ravens are here to tell you that this union is magical."

Well, that sure was a unique way to look at it. Because I am not completely familiar with the Native American beliefs, I had never looked at it this way.

Our ceremony went off without a hitch, except, of course, for the one between the two of us. After all, we were getting remarried! It was beautiful. It was perfect just the way it was and the best thing about it was that I was reminded of one of life's truths.

There is always a gift in everything. It's just how we look at it. It's like that old saying about seeing the cup half full, rather than half empty. We had started out our day in a negative way, but then we were reminded to see the gift. The gift is that everything is perfect in itself. . .good, bad or otherwise. It's just a matter of how we choose to see it.

Thoughts for Your Journey

Listen to yourself and be aware of when you are running negativity. Know that in every situation there is something positive to see. Write about your discoveries.

Take some time to think about someone or something that you find fault with. Now find at least one thing positive about them or it. For instance, I used to blame my husband for everything. It wasn't until I started looking for the positive things about him and finding gratitude for him that the walls came tumbling down. See where there is negativity and blame in your life. This could be in different situations. It could be with your spouse, it could be with your boss, with your co-workers, or other family members. It could be just with how you see your day-to-day life in general. Write your thoughts and feelings.

THE ANSWERS YOU SEEK COME FROM WITHIN

Our trip to Sedona has sadly come to an end. It is time to go home. But I leave here having taken another step towards wholeness.

I came to Sedona looking for answers. Part of me was still searching on the outside to fill the hole within. I thought by spending time with the Indians here I would discover my truth. I did, but not the way I expected.

Because the Hopi Indians are such a peaceful people, I knew they must have the answer to discovering a peace within. Over the last few days, we went to the Hopi Reservation to visit in their homes and we also went into the woods to experience Indian ceremonies. The Hopis are wonderful people, but after spending time with them, I realize they are no different thank you or me. They have a peaceful way about them and they live in harmony with the land, but they still have issues. They are human, too. I guess I thought they were beyond the rest of us. But they aren't.

So I continue my journey home having been reminded that the truth is not found somewhere on the outside. It comes from within. No one has the answers for me. No one can tell me my truth. I am the only one who knows it, for it is in my heart. I can read books, I can hear speakers, and I can experience all different kinds of people, but my truth lies within because that's where the love lives.

This is one more step to wholeness. I know first hand that I have to go within.

Thoughts for Your Journey

Books, classes, tapes, and other people's ways are all mediums for you to contemplate what you believe for your spiritual truth. Then you have to go within and see what rings true for you. What are your spiritual beliefs?

After looking at your spiritual beliefs, are you "buying into" someone else's ideas that don't ring true for you? Is the little child in you working from a place of fear in these beliefs or from a place of love? Ask yourself these questions and discover what rings true to your heart.

EMBRACE THE JOURNEY

There is a meadow. In this meadow are the most beautiful colors I have ever seen: yellows, lavenders, oranges, and pinks. They are the colors of spring. The sun highlights everything, including the woman I see. She glides through the meadow in a flowing white gown with peace and love emanating from her. This is a portrait. . .a picture of how I want to be.

I realize this is a picture I have painted for myself as I am in a coaching session with a friend. I see the painting for her and realize it is a message for me, too. I recognize that even though I thought I was accepting myself and loving myself unconditionally, in reality I was still painting a perfect picture of spirituality. And I was trying to accelerate the process. In my mind, that painting was my goal, but what I was saying to myself was that I was not accepting my process of getting there. I was not accepting me.

As you make the choice to become aware of your spiritual journey. . .we are all on one. . . some just choose to be in denial about it. . .please, remember that it is the journey that is important. It is fine to have a goal. My goal for this lifetime is to love unconditionally. However, I realize now that to truly love with no judgment, I have to love the process. And that means that I have to love my humanness and my mistakes. I have to find a space of forgiveness for myself.

Ironically, as I move into this awareness, I feel I am finally getting it. I thought I was all along, but now I am seeing me, accepting me and loving me just for who I am right now in the present moment.

The key is not to try and achieve. . .the key is simply to forgive yourself. . .to allow yourself to be.

Thoughts for Your Journey

Are you trying to accelerate yourself through the process of healing? If you are, then you most likely have not forgiven yourself for who you are right now. What judgments are you putting on yourself that hold you back? Remember that to truly move into wholeness, you must forgive and accept where you are right now. Spend some time with this and then write your findings.

Write ten things about yourself that you are thankful for right now.

QUIETING THE CHATTER

"Silence is golden." How many times have we all heard that phrase? I always thought of it only as quieting the noise around me. Now I'm beginning to realize that it also means for me to quiet the noise in my head.

Last night I woke up in the middle of the night itching. A few days ago at the beach I got so into my writing that I rolled over onto my stomach and proceeded to fry my back to a nice tomato red. I haven't done that in fifteen years. I am paying for it now. So my skin is now in that horrible itching stage of trying to heal. I have tried to calm it down, but nothing seemed to help. That is, until I awoke at three this morning.

In the silence of the night and in the quietness of my brain, when I found myself scratching, I asked, "How do I make this go away?"

The answer was so clear. I heard myself say to take an antihistamine. I would never have considered that as an answer, but I decided to try it. Lo and behold, it worked! I can't explain why, but I do know that the itching subsided. Maybe I made it happen with my mind. Maybe some would say it was just a coincidence. Or maybe it was my truth. I believe that was the answer. . .it was my truth.

How many times have you discovered your truth in the middle of the night? I often hear people say they wake up from a dead sleep to find answers they have been in search of. That is because their minds are quiet. The chatter has slowed down enough for them to hear their truth.

I have dreams that are like movies and they always give me information on my inner truth. I now realize that they have been a way for God to talk to me because my mind has always tried to analyze everything. . .so much so that I couldn't hear

 Message Sent 83

my truth. Now don't get me wrong, when I meditate I can hear the answers and when I directly ask something from God, I feel I often get an answer. But I want to get my answers and be awake at the same time. Isn't that a provocative thought. . .to be anywhere at anytime and be able to go into my knowingness and find my answers.

I know the reason I have so much chatter in my mind is because I don't fully trust myself. I trust God, but not myself. The irony of this is that I know God is everywhere and everything, including me. The spirit is inside of me and, yet, I always think of it as outside, detached from me.

"I trust God and I trust myself, because God is within me. God is the knowingness, the peace, and the calm. God is the love that is in abundance everywhere, including within me. God is my truth."

This is my belief. Now I must "own it" and become one with it. I feel so excited and grateful to finally be aware of this. I know me well enough now that I will allow myself the time to integrate this into my being. I'm like a child all over again. . .finding the wonder in life and feeling the excitement for having discovered it!

Thoughts for Your Journey

Do you trust yourself enough to allow your mind to be silent? Or do your fears keep your mind busy? What feelings surface for you after reading this entry?

Are your dreams trying to send messages to you? Listen to your dreams to see if they have any meaning for you. If you can't remember your dreams, then ask God to guide you into a space so that you can receive the messages. Remember that "silence is golden." Give yourself some time today to sit in silence. Write any discoveries.

You Don't Have to Make Everyone Happy

"You are not to blame for your mother's pain." These words stopped me in my tracks today as I was about to give my mom a healing. I asked, "What?" Again, I heard in my head, "You are not to blame for your mother's pain."

Mom is visiting me while recuperating from the stroke she had recently. I want to help her heal. When I heard these words ringing in my ears, I was dumbfounded. I never thought of myself as feeling responsible for any of my mother's pain, but in that moment, I knew I had lived my whole life as if it were the truth.

I don't know when, as a child, I took that responsibility on, but as I flash back through the years, I see how I've tried to make her happy and to heal her. This has been mostly in my adult years, because during my teenage ones we fought too much. I was angry and didn't really care to make her happy, or anyone else for that matter.

Now I see all of the times I've given her material goods. I thought I was doing it partially because I felt guilty for having so much when she didn't and partially because I wanted her to know I loved her. That was part of it, but now I believe I've hit the nail on the head. The little girl inside of me thought she was bad and felt guilty for it and, as a result, wanted to win her mother's approval.

What freedom to finally see this. My mom and I have had an open conversation over the past few years and I felt as if I had forgiven her and myself. However, I have continually found myself in resistance to her when we are face to face. I didn't understand this, until now. The little girl inside of me felt like a very bad person. I'm not sure why, probably due to some trivial event in our lives that meant nothing to my mother, but meant everything to me. And as a result, I built my whole life feeling responsible for making her happy.

"You two are making me crazy!" I remember screaming these words at my kids recently. I finally realize that these are the trivial things that make my children feel responsible for me. I can't believe I've been doing this. I know that no one can make me crazy. I choose to stay in a situation and feel that way, and, yet, I've been sending my kids the message that they are responsible for my happiness and my sanity.

No one is responsible for my happiness and I am not responsible for anyone else's. What a relief to see this. I know I am responsible for taking care of my children, feeding them, sheltering them, nurturing them and being an example to them; however, I am not responsible for making them happy. I realize I have been trying to make them happy since their births and A.J. since he was almost five. More often than not I am frustrated and guilt-ridden because I feel as if I haven't done a good enough job. Now I know it's because I've been carrying around a negative charge that tells me that I am responsible for people's happiness.

These responsibility feelings have kept me from totally being in my truth, not only with my mom and my kids, but, also, with my husband and friends. I have been afraid to say exactly how I feel because I don't want to hurt anyone. And the irony is that I have hurt people because I can't help but communicate my feelings. I have tried to hold them in to make others happy, but then I explode. The end result is usually an angry battle that probably never would have happened if I had been honest in the first place.

I held myself back in my work, also, because of this responsibility issue. I limited myself with work because I felt I had to be involved in every aspect of my kids' lives to make sure they were happy. I feared that if I didn't make them happy, they would judge me and not love me. It's funny, for a long time I could see this for clients, but I didn't see it for myself so much.

I had a client who was angry at life because she wasn't fulfilled. She wanted a part-time career, but felt guilty about not being with her kids all of the time. I asked her to take a look at two scenarios. One was for her to live a life of anger and frustration because she was unfulfilled, taking it out on her kids. Not only would she be sending the kids a message that she was unhappy and they were part of the reason why, but, also, when they grow up, they will have the same misery because that is the example she has set.

The other scenario was for her to create a career where she is happy and fulfilled. She would come home to her kids at night and give them quality time that would let them know she loves them. She would live her life powerfully and full of love and, at the same time, set an example, giving her kids permission to do the same. I asked her which one she would choose. She opted for this one.

I do, too! I choose to live powerfully. By allowing this, I am choosing to take care of myself and to love myself. I am being an example of truth.

After receiving all of the wonderful gifts of insight today, I decided to give my children a gift tonight. "I want you to know that you are not responsible for my happiness. Sometimes, I say things like 'you're making me nuts.' I want you to know how sorry I am for making you guys feel responsible for me. You can only make yourselves happy. We all have to choose to be happy. And when I say something like that I now realize that I am choosing to be a victim and not take care of myself and be responsible for myself."

Kolbi responded with, "Mom does that mean I don't have to kiss and hug you anymore at school with all of those people around?"

I think she got it!

What better message can I give my children and the ones around me than this: none of us is responsible for another's happiness. Our responsibility to the world around us is to find happiness within ourselves. Once we take responsibility for ourselves, live in our truths, and choose to live powerfully, then our examples allow others to do the same. Living powerfully doesn't mean that you have to go out and conquer the world. It simply means that you are doing what feels right in your heart. For some this may mean being a handyman or an executive, for others it may mean being a mom or a nurse. The end result for each of us who chooses to live powerfully is unconditional love for ourselves, and the world around us.

Thoughts for Your Journey

When you read this entry, what responsibility pictures come to your mind? Do you put too much responsibility on yourself for your family, your friends, or co-workers? Or are you the victim who makes everyone else responsible for your happiness?

Responsibility for others tends to bury us in guilt. Sit quietly and go into a meditative place and ask yourself if this rings true for you. If it does and you are ready to let go of the guilt, then ask God to help you release this pain. If the guilt is not yet ready to go away, accept this and allow yourself to be in it. Ask for the gift of this situation and give thanks.

SURROUND YOURSELF WITH LOVE

"I can't do this anymore! You always make me feel like I'm wrong for how I do things. I'm done!" I slammed down the telephone and screamed at the top of my lungs. I have had enough. I have put up with this unloving relationship for way too long.

Every time Lisa and I talk, she proceeds to blast me with her viewpoints so heavily that I feel like a tiny little girl being reprimanded. Now, obviously, this is her issue about needing to control me into her way of thinking, but I've put up with it for so long that I start shaking inside every time we talk. I know it's because I haven't stood up for myself. I have walked on eggshells with her for years for fear if I didn't conform to her way of thinking, then our friendship would end. I guess, subconsciously, I felt it was the only kind of relationship I deserved.

This incident just happened on the day my mom left from visiting. I realized while doing some healing work on my mom that she has really felt alone in this life and felt very unloved as a little girl. I feel great compassion for her.

My relationship with Lisa is working out a lot of the issues with my mom. I felt my mom's controls on me very much as a child. I'll never forget the time she forced me to kiss my little sister when we were fighting. Mom tends to take up for the other person because she doesn't like conflict. She doesn't feel the freedom to express herself. I understand this now. On the other hand, because I felt she didn't take up for me, nor did I ever see her take a stand for herself, I didn't give me permission to take up for myself. Or if I did, it was usually in a very angry way, sort of like with Lisa.

I hung on to my friendship with Lisa because I hoped she would be able to love me for who I am. I know she is having a hard time with the changes I've made in my life over the past few years. And I know that she is in fear. I can accept that. I thought to be spiritual, though, that I had to love her unconditionally. This is true; however, I have to love myself unconditionally first. I can accept her for where she is on her journey, but that doesn't mean I have to continually be abused because of it. This is taking a stand in my truth. As I allow myself to take this stand, the anger dissipates.

I get it! My anger is not with Lisa, but with myself. I am angry for not having stood up for me all along. She has her issues and I have mine. For me to find a space of love in my heart for her, I have to honor the little girl inside of me first. I have to let her know she is loved and valued and doesn't have to be in an unhealthy relationship. What a revelation! I can take care of me and honor my needs. I am worthy of being loved. And with this insight, I find gratitude for Lisa for helping me to find my truth and then wish her well on her journey.

I always hear people say, "become a part of the we," meaning to be at one with everyone else. However, I now understand that the "we" inside of me has to be whole first. I'm talking about loving all of the parts of me that make up my whole. I'm talking about standing up for myself, but not having to push it down anyone's throat. I'm talking about accepting me as I am and loving those who don't, but not having to surround myself with them. I thought I had to keep Lisa in my life to learn some great lesson. Well, I finally have. I love me enough to stand up for myself and surround myself with love.

Thoughts for Your Journey

Do you surround yourself with love? Are you giving it to yourself? If you don't stand up for yourself and love yourself, then nobody will. Feel any pain and guilt that comes up for you. Write your discoveries.

What changes can you make in your life right now to surround yourself with more love? What holds you back from doing this? If you are in fear, ask God to help you face this. Remember to turn over the reins when you can. This is turning to trust.

THE "HOKEY-POKEY DANCE"
OF TRUST

Imagine a sculptor chipping away at the biggest, most beautiful piece of marble. It can be any color. He is creating a masterpiece. This sculptor is you; only you are not a sculptor. You are just you...human. So now the job becomes more tedious. It could take hours, days, months, maybe even years...possibly a lifetime.

The ego is the reason we struggle with revealing our masterpieces. The ego is our humanness. It's our fears, our wants, our desires, and our needs. I'm talking about the part of us that keeps us from being in total service to God. I'm talking about the part that continues to make us feel separate. The ego is the part of us that continues to play mental games even when we think we are finally letting go.

A friend of mine was recently working through some of her own issues. She didn't realize it, but she was throwing some very negative remarks around and was withdrawing from the world, which included me. At first I handled it very well. I was grounded in my truth and felt completely connected to God and the world around me. But then, as the days ticked by, I started playing mental games with myself. "Do I call her and ask what's going on? Did I do something to create this separation?" My heart knew what was going on, but my head wouldn't listen.

These questions began to nag at me. Pretty soon, I lost my truth. I began to drag another friend, Patty, into the mix and ask her opinions. Every time I talked to Patty for the next few days I dragged her into conversations lamenting the woes of me and what to do. Before long, I had stepped back in time to when I was a little child feeling lost and alone. I had created a mental war with my ego and I was losing.

"I'm done, Patty. I don't have to do this anymore." The light was finally starting to come back on. For a while, I was completely lost in that darkness. I was the one who chose to let my friend's journey get to me. That was my ego getting in the way again for fear it wasn't going to be loved. But it is loved. God loves the complete me. I'm the one who was playing these games.

It's a day or so later, Mother's Day, and I am listening to my mom's pain. She feels hurt by her fiancè because she feels he wasn't nice enough to her on this special day. She goes on and on for at least ten minutes complaining. I find myself frustrated. We have these kinds of conversations often. I just want my mom to find some happiness and not keep doing these mental games with herself. I know the little girl inside of her is in great pain.

A day later, I'm wishing Patty a belated Happy Mother's Day. We are catching up. I tell her about my mom and how I wish she would choose to heal herself and how I wish I could accept her constant complaining and mental games. "It gets so old," I tell her. And she replies, "Yes, it sure does."

Oh, boy! Just that little response from Patty hit me like a lightning bolt. I was doing the mental games like my mom. We all have a tendency to do it. But in that single moment, I saw myself so clearly and knew that I had to heal this part of my ego. Just being aware of it has already started the process. Now, when I begin the mental war, I stop. I take a breath and tell myself that I don't have to go there. I say to myself "Know your truth, Terri. Trust yourself. You are fine just the way you are. You are already a masterpiece. We all are."

I like to call this going in and out of the ego the "Hokey-Pokey Dance of Trust." Some days you put your foot in and the next day, the foot comes right back out. And then there are those days when you put your whole body into trust and then there are the days you don't. You feel so completely connected to spirit when you have jumped in with your whole body and let the ego go. That's when you truly feel like "dancing all about." As for me, I have days when I feel completely in that dance and then the next moment I won't. All in the same day!

The whole point is for us to try to remember that life is a dance and we're all doing it. Somehow by realizing this, it allows us to be forgiving of our humanness. . .allowing us, the sculptors, to continue the rhythm of our work.

Thoughts for Your Journey

Is your ego playing games with you? What keeps you from being in trust?

Give yourself permission to be human today. Make this your awareness. Every time you begin to play mental games with yourself, stop, take a breath, forgive yourself and become aware of your fear. After all, fear is the culprit behind these mental games. Give thanks for each situation that brings you into this awareness. The situation is allowing you to heal. Write how you feel about yourself after spending a day in this awareness.

TAKE BACK THE AUTHORITY IN YOUR LIFE

My body trembles. I laugh out of nervousness. My dentist consoles me and assures me that there is nothing to worry about. I am about to have a root canal.

Where is my sense of peace and calm? I have been a nervous wreck for two days, ever since he dumped the bad news on me. The pain I was experiencing definitely called for a root canal. Not my idea of fun.

As I settle down with numbness taking over, I try to convince myself that this is going to be no big deal. Everyone else has told me just the opposite, but, nonetheless, I am trying to stay within my own experience and not buy into what others say.

I have been asking myself since I received the bad news, "Why have I brought this to my life?" I haven't been able to get an answer. Now I think I know it. You see, this morning I called my doctor to tell him I was considering having a specialist do the procedure rather than him. He, of course, told me it was my choice. He reassured me he could do the job; he does them every day. He did say, however, that if he got into the roots and saw that I fell within that two percent of the population where I needed "extra help," then he would send me on my way.

Well, I just got the boot. I'm in that two percent and after digging around in my roots, my doctor says I need to see a specialist.

Why didn't I listen to my gut? It told me to call a specialist. Even my husband and friends told me to. As I look at this and ask myself "Why?" I get the answer that once again I was thinking of what someone else needed, rather than myself. In this case I didn't want to hurt my doctor's feelings because he's a friend. I didn't want him to feel that I didn't trust him by going to see a specialist in the first place. Now I need to have a root canal all over again!

I put my trust in my doctor, when all along I should have put it in myself. Yes, I do believe we need to trust in the people around us, especially the doctors who work on us. But more importantly, when my gut overrides what my head is telling me I should do, then it's time for me to listen.

I get little tests every day to trust myself if I'll just listen. I know when I don't listen it's because of that little child inside of me who's been told that people in authority know best. In some cases they do. But it's important for me to always check in with that little girl first. She's the one who knows my truth.

Thoughts for Your Journey

Are you listening to your gut? Or do you give your power over to authority figures? What rings true for you here?

If you disown yourself, then you are in fear. What keeps you from trusting your intuition? Why do you give others' opinions the authority in your life? Ask the little child within what memories surface for you.

MISTRUST

It is the day before my stepson, A.J., will be leaving on a campout. This campout will consist of four guys and four girls. It is in celebration of A.J.'s seventeenth birthday. There will be no adults tagging along. Needless to say, I am dealing with myself.

"A.J. don't you dare screw up. You know if you do anything wrong, that's it!"

"I know, Ter, we're not going to get into any trouble." A.J. is trying to console me, as well as his dad. He just came into our room to say goodnight and we're blasting him. "Why are you guys getting so mad? You said I could go."

Yes, indeed, why are we getting so mad? When I ask God for guidance on this I am told it is because I am in fear, not so much fear that A.J. might get into trouble, but fear that if he does get into trouble, I won't be able to trust myself to handle the ramifications. It's that little girl inside of me feeling overwhelmed and not sure what to do.

God reminds me that A.J. is a wonderful spirit and has never been in any kind of trouble. He is very open with us and always lets us know what is going on with him so we won't worry. He tells us just about everything. . .and I mean everything!

Many parents would not want to hear a kid say the things A.J. tells us. He's done this forever. I can even remember when he was in the sixth grade and went to summer camp. He sent us postcards telling us he was learning to French kiss. That was just as an eleven-year-old. You can imagine what he must be like as a junior in high school. My point is that he is a well-rounded young man and we have a wonderful communicative relationship. I'm not naive, however, so I do know there are things that are not meant for his dad's or my ears. This is where the mistrust comes in. But once again, I am assured that it is a mistrust of myself.

"God, have we set a good enough example for A.J.? Will he make the right choices?" I question this and again I am reminded of what I already know as truth.

God tells me, "A.J. is on his own journey. His life is his creation. If you try to control him out of your own fears, then he will move into resistance. Resistance is a form of fear. And, of course, if he works out of fear, then he cannot be in trust. Fear is the opposite of trust."

We want A.J. to live in trust, not fear. Sometimes we just get in the way a little. It's not because we want to control him or to berate him. It really just comes down to how much we love and trust ourselves to allow him to be on his own spiritual journey. Because the reality of it is this: even if he should make a poor decision, insight and wisdom will still be gained. In fact, some of the best lessons that make an impact on us are the hard ones. They are the ones that we live to tell about. . .the ones that we survive and grow from.

This talk with God is a powerful one for me. I flash back on the times when I was in resistance with A.J. and can see my fear. . .fear of letting go and letting God take over. It was fear of losing control, not control of A.J., but control of myself. I didn't trust myself to handle whatever might come along, be it judgment, more responsibilities on my shoulders, or you name it. We've all seen how teenagers' choices affect their own lives and their parents'. The whole family's world can be turned upside down. I was afraid of this and that is why I had the need to control.

I can let go of the shackles that keep me bound in control. A.J. is his own unique individual and if we allow him to be just that, then he will discover his truth and live powerfully. What more could a parent ask for?

After this wonderful conversation with God and after being reminded of why we are all here. . .to be on our own journeys, I find some peace to fall asleep on. I can let go. And with that, I can send A.J. on his way to having a wonderful birthday.

Thoughts for Your Journey

Do you find yourself controlling a situation because you mistrust yourself? What fears come up for you after reading this journal entry?

Give thanks for this reflection of your fears. Remember, you can turn the reins of your life over to trust at anytime. What keeps you from doing this right now?

WHO ARE YOU COMPETING WITH?

June gloom has descended upon Southern California. It's Sunday afternoon. It is the perfect kind of day to relax, but I can't.

A mental war takes over my life again. There is something inside of me that says I am supposed to be up and moving. I am supposed to be productive. . .creating something. Where does this mental tug-of-war come from? My heart says relax, but my head says get moving.

I decide to take a look at what is driving me. This is not just a one-day battle within. This is an ongoing war of wits. Will my heart win? Or will my head win? I have to go within to see what this mega force is inside my head that keeps me from "being."

It is society. Society says we have to constantly keep moving up. Whether it's with our work, with how we look or how much money we have. . .we have to be competitive. But with whom am I competing? I am a mom and wife first, a spiritual coach, and now a writer. There is no one with whom I am competing. I am the one buying into this paranoia. What's wrong with just being me? Am I still seeking outside acknowledgment? Am I still looking for approval from the outside, rather than from within? I know in my heart that if the only thing I ever do is to be a "light unto the darkness" for those around me, then I have fulfilled my destiny.

"Please, God, show me the way to be a light. Show me how to serve you, not what society says I should do. Help me to accept the person I am right now. Please help me to receive your love. I open my heart to you."

Thoughts for Your Journey

Do you feel as if you are competing with the world, always trying to win? Who are you competing with? Write your thoughts and feelings.

Give yourself permission to be you today. Every time you find yourself competing with someone, stop yourself. Then ask your inner child how he or she really feels and act upon the message that is revealed.

Are You Buried in Responsibilities?

Control is a fear. I finally realize why I am controlling with so many things in my life. I feel responsible for everything around me. This puts me into fear.

I went on a field trip today with Kolbi's class and what I came home with was a new awareness. I have shared before that I feel quite a bit of anxiety around her teacher. That's because she is very controlling. I know she is a reflection to my own pain. She controls and then I want to control. If I didn't have issues with this, she wouldn't bother me. Remember, everything and everyone that we react to is a reflection to our fear and pain.

We visited a beautiful botanical garden with another class. As the trip came to a close, we had lunch on the picnic grounds by the parking lot. The other teacher's class ran around, skipping and playing through the trees. Ours, on the other hand, was told to sit down. Our kids were confined to their seats. They weren't even allowed to explore through the trees like the other class.

Everyone noticed what was going on. The mothers in our group discussed how unfair this seemed. We talked about how controlling this teacher can be.

Then the miracle happened. One of our kids couldn't sit still any longer and started to run around. Kolbi's teacher grabbed him and told him to sit down. She said, "I feel so responsible for all of you. I don't want you to get hurt." She was being controlling out of her fear of feeling so responsible for all of the kids' safety.

That's when the gift came to me. This is why I am so

controlling. I feel responsible for everything around me. I stay in fear. Whether I feel responsible for my kids, my mom, my husband, or my friends, it all makes me want to control. My responsibility issues surface and I want to control because I feel I am supposed to protect everyone and make him or her happy. I feel responsible for everyone's life and as a result, I forget my own. I fear that I won't do my job good enough. I fear that I will let people down and then they won't accept me. I fear they won't love me. I fear they will reject me.

This all plays into my perfect pictures again. . .pictures of how I "think" I am supposed to be. Well, after today, I realize that I can only be me. I am just one person. I cannot make everyone around me fulfilled and happy. I can't protect them from life's hurts.

The ones I can only attempt to protect are my children. And that is mostly with safety issues. I can also continue to show them tools to empower themselves. But that is all I can really do. My responsibility is to give them an example to follow, but at some point I have to turn to trust.

Like today, before my epiphany, if I had been the teacher in this situation, I probably would have let the kids run around, but I most likely would have been filled with concern and fear for them. However, if I knew then what I know now, I believe I would have set boundaries for the kids to stay away from the parking lot, but I would have allowed them some space to run and explore. And then I would let myself relax. This would be an act of trust. I have to believe that each child, each person, is on his or her own journey and I can't control his or her destiny. I am not responsible for everyone's choices.

I understand this now. What a great gift Kolbi's teacher has been to me this year. I have learned so much through her fears. To my amazement, I find myself feeling more and more compassion for her. . .and for myself.

If I am to let go of these responsibility fears and to release the controls of everyone's lives, then I must forgive myself. I must forgive me for not being able to live up to the perfect pictures I've painted for myself. And then I must turn to trust.

Thoughts for Your Journey

In what areas of your life do you feel too much responsibility? Are you afraid of not being loved? Are you afraid of being rejected? Go deep within to find out what keeps you hanging onto the controls of others' lives.

Go into awareness during interactions with others and see when you are feeling responsible for their happiness. Ask yourself what you need to do to release these feelings. Write about your discoveries.

LET GO OF THE "SHOULDS"

Time is not my enemy. Time is my friend. . .if I allow it to be. I choose to live life more passionately.

For years I found myself racing against the clock, usually trying to make sure that I didn't screw up something. Whether it was a fear of being late getting my kids to school for fear their teacher would judge me, or whether I was afraid of not getting everything done that I felt should be done, I constantly raced. My body raced, my heart raced, my mind raced. Nothing stayed in the moment when I felt I had to make everyone happy.

These are the "shoulds." I "should" do this, I "should've" done that. It all plays into that perfect picture of how we "should" be. I've done this my whole life. Now I'm letting those pictures go.

"Mackenzie is quitting her hip hop class. She's tired and bored from it. I don't want her to live her life that way. I want her to do things that she feels passionately about."

I got raked across the coals for making that statement to a friend. She gave me a five-minute dissertation on why we should make our kids be committed to things and not be allowed to quit. I told her I used to feel the same way until I decided I wanted to quit my dance class, too. I was also bored. I was kind of dealing with myself about it because I've always heard people say it is wrong to quit anything. "Don't be a quitter." How many times have we all heard that? Then I decided to meditate on this and I received my answer.

Our world is stuck in mediocrity because people are living their lives doing what they think they "should" do, rather than what makes them feel passionately. Of course, there are some things that go along with our jobs or with parenting that we don't necessarily enjoy, but because the overall job brings us great satisfaction, then we do those little things that are annoying. But if the whole job is annoying, then a shift is needed. You have to take a look at what is bothering you and heal that part of you that is hurting. As far as extracurricular activities go, if it's something that doesn't make you feel alive, then you are doing no one any good to be there, especially you, just because you feel you "should" stick to your commitment.

I believe these "shoulds" that are ingrained in us since childhood are a big part of the reason we don't know ourselves. They are why we don't trust ourselves to listen to our inner voice. That's because we were never allowed to trust it before. Most of us have been told for so long how we should feel and what we should do that we don't even know our truths. It's like a parent telling a child that they have to put a coat on because the parent says it is cold. The kid fights and fights with this, because he or she doesn't feel cold. But the parent wins out, of course, and before long the child loses out. Not only does the child lose this battle of wits, but he or she also loses the sense of self. The child begins to lose trust in his or her knowingness.

This is why it is so important for us to start breaking the tradition of the "shoulds." Imagine what the world would be like if people took time to get to know themselves, to get out of the "shoulds," to find what makes them feel passionately. If we all lived in a way that really made us feel "awake" every day, then this world would be a more loving and forgiving place.

This is why time is no longer my enemy. It was only my enemy because I found myself doing things that kept me in a constant state of the "shoulds". . .but not anymore. I can no longer live my life for what I think I should do. I have to live it passionately, being in my truth. The little girl inside of me is jumping for joy and so are my kids, for that matter. By living my life passionately, I set an example for my children, as well as others around me. I set an example of living powerfully and standing in my truth.

Thoughts for Your Journey

Go into an awareness today of the "shoulds." Every time you catch yourself saying this word or thinking it, stop yourself. Ask yourself what you would really like to do or not do, instead of what you should or shouldn't do. Write down your discoveries.

What are you afraid of? What fears that you discovered about yourself are keeping you in the "shoulds?" If you are having trouble tapping into the fears, then go into your meditation garden again and talk to the little child inside of you. Ask the child what he or she is afraid of. See if you can forgive yourself for holding onto these fears. If you can't, that is okay. Remind yourself that this, too, will pass.

BE HONEST WITH YOURSELF

"Mommy p-l-e-a-s-e put me to bed. I want you Mommy!" Kolbi is sobbing. She's actually throwing a tantrum, which I've never seen her do before. Just five minutes prior to this antic, I asked her to let me put Mackenzie to bed this night. I spent the whole day with Kolbi on a school field trip and then took her horseback riding in the afternoon. I needed a little time with Mackenzie. It was supposed to be Kolbi's night for me to put her to bed, but since I spent so much time with her today and none with Mackenzie, I asked her to switch tonight and she had said "yes." That is until the tantrum began.

"Kolbi, what about me? You're making me feel bad." That's the little boy inside of my husband, Steve, speaking out. Now his feelings are getting hurt, because he came to put Kolbi to bed and she wants me. This is a no-win situation, but I can't hear him say this to her. His words tell Kolbi that she is responsible for her Dad's feelings. I don't want this message sent to our kids.

"Kolbi, you are not responsible for your Dad's feelings and you're not responsible for mine. On the other hand, it is not my job to make you happy, just as it's not your job to make anyone else happy. You have to be true to yourself. Honey, I asked you five minutes ago if I could put Mackenzie to bed and you said yes. Why are you upset now?"

Kolbi can barely speak; she is crying so hard. "Mommy, I told you it was okay to put Mackenzie to bed because I didn't want her to feel sad. But now, I really want you to put me to bed."

Kolbi's reply stops me in my tracks. I see myself as a little kid when I didn't think I could say or feel what I needed, because I thought everyone else had to come first. It's okay to put others first as long as you don't feel angry about doing it. When you feel angry about it, you build a wedge between you and that other person and create resentment. You have to speak your truth. Ironically, when you do start to speak your truth and don't judge yourself for it, the compassion comes and then often an agreement can be made where everyone is happy. That's because you are in a space of truth and love.

"Kolbi, honey, I am so sorry you feel so bad. If you had told me from the start how you felt then I would have definitely stuck to our original plan. However, since I already told Mackenzie that I am putting her to bed, I am going to stick to it."

"Mommy, please." Kolbi's body screams with anger. She thinks she is mad at me, but I can tell she is really mad at herself. She knows I am speaking the truth.

"Kolbi, I love you honey, but I am not going to take back what I have already promised Mackenzie. I would like to ask, from now on, for you to be honest with yourself about what feels right for you. If you do that from the beginning then things like this won't happen. It is perfectly all right for you to take care of your feelings. As I said, it is not your responsibility to make Mackenzie happy, or anyone else for that matter."

And with that, Kolbi came up and hugged me. She now had permission to be in her truth. I feel this is the greatest gift I can ever give her.

As I reflect on all of this, I see how my whole life was driven by what would make other people happy and what I felt would get me approval. I didn't trust myself enough to stand in my truth. But now I do.

Thoughts for Your Journey

Are you speaking your honest feelings to others? Or are you holding back your words out of some fear or some concern? Are you giving up yourself and burying the pain? Be honest with yourself and write your feelings.

It's time to forgive yourself for not taking care of the little child within you. It's time to take responsibility for your little child within and stop neglecting him or her! You don't have to give yourself up anymore. Remember that by honoring yourself, it is easier to honor and love others. How would your life be different if you took care of the child's feelings inside of you as much as you take care of everyone else's?

PROTECT YOUR LITTLE CHILD WITHIN

It is the most glorious day outside. It is Memorial Day Weekend and the beach is not too packed to enjoy, but has just enough people on it to let you know that summer is finally here. Steve and I watch Kolbi and a friend dig for sand crabs. It is the perfect beach day.

That is until this cute little blonde girl comes toddling along. Steve and I laugh at her curiosity. She has sunglasses on. They are the ones with the double lenses so that you can open the dark lenses to the side and it looks like you have on reading glasses. She looks up at the sky and down at the sand to see how they look with the glasses open and then with them shut. She is completely at home in her two-year-old world.

"Steve, no one is looking after this little girl." My voice rises an octave or so as I watch her make her way further down the beach. My heart races. "Where is her mom? Who's looking after her? Doesn't anyone see that she's alone? Steve, I'm going to follow her. I can't believe no one is going after her!" I am on my way. I don't want to make a scene with this little girl and I definitely do not want to frighten her. But the momma lioness is awake and is in protective mode.

This little beach bunny is now a hundred yards from where I originally saw her. I go up to her and ask her name. She says "no" and runs off. I do this two more times with her and still have no luck. I am torn as to how to handle this. A friend I see on the beach suggests that I go to the lifeguard. Great idea, but she has to keep an eye on the kid. I'm not about to let her out of my sight.

Just as I make my way up to the lifeguard stand, another

lifeguard drives up and yells at me that the little girl's mom is looking for her. My husband let him know that I am on her trail. I go up to the little girl and tell her I want to take her to her mommy. No problem with that. It's almost too easy to get her up into my arms, but I am nonetheless thankful that she isn't hysterical.

We climb into the lifeguard's truck and make our way down the beach. A beautiful blonde woman stands there waiting on us. I jump out of the truck and ask her if she is okay. She tells me that she is not the child's mom, she is just a neighbor watching her, and proceeds to reprimand this little two-year-old for wandering off. I am in shock, but at the same time I know in my heart that she is truly shaken and this is the only way she knows how to handle the situation.

Life is back to normal and I've found my way back to our beach blanket. I congratulate myself for not blasting the woman who I thought was the little girl's mom. I know in the past, maybe even as recently as six months ago, I would have jumped out of that truck and probably yelled at her for not paying better attention. But, to my surprise, I asked her if she was okay. Because I have been forgiving myself for my own mistakes, it came as second nature to have compassion and forgiveness for her. With that you might think I would feel great comfort and peace for watching over this little child and getting her to safety, but I don't. I can hardly breathe. My chest and my throat are so tight. I can't get them to release.

It is now four days later and these feelings still haunt me. What gift did this little girl's spirit bring for me to see? What has she shown me that needs to be healed in my life?

I sink into a deep meditation. The answers are finally here. The little girl inside of me never felt totally protected. My mom wanted me to conform because that's how the little girl inside of her saw that people got acceptance and my dad didn't mind if I was "me" as long as it went along with his point of view. Neither one of them loved themselves enough to live truthfully, for fear they wouldn't be accepted. By making me act a certain way, they both thought they were protecting me. I know they did this out of love for me. They both had their views on what would give me the least resistance and pain along the way. The only problem with this, though, was that they weren't protecting the unique little being that I already was. Therefore, I didn't feel protected. Instead I felt attacked. I understand and forgive all of this. I know my parents were trying to do what they thought was best for me and I love them so much for that. They were trying to keep me from pain.

Now, as I've finally gotten some closure on this, I realize once again that it is up to me to take care of and protect myself. By protecting myself, I mean to believe in myself, stand up for myself and to have faith in God. It's up to me to protect myself by continuing to heal the pain.

Thoughts for Your Journey

Are you protecting the little child within you? Feel any emotions that are coming up for you and then write down your findings.

What can you do today to start protecting yourself and the little child within?

MIRACLES CAN HAPPEN TO YOU

"Terri, I love you."

"What?" I ask.

"Terri, I love you!"

I was in church tonight with my friends, Patty and Renee. We were in the middle of a meditation and I heard these words. Only these words were in my thoughts. No one around me was talking to me...at least not anyone in the physical sense.

"Who's there? I can't see you. Please, come around to the front of me so that I may see you." My eyes were closed and, yet, I saw this vision. I see pictures in my mind's eye constantly. We all do. It's just like envisioning in your mind an old friend. You can see the person with your eyes closed.

"Who are you? Please, come so that I may see you." I felt the presence move around to the front of me. Tears rolled down my face. It was the presence of God in the form of Jesus. I felt as if my hands were taken into his. He told me "Thank you. Thank you, Terri, for stepping up to the plate. You are doing good work and we are so proud of you." I felt angels all around me. I felt them touching me and filling me up with love.

I was speechless. I was given a message tonight that I am on the right path. I have felt this in my heart. What a gift to see this. But did I imagine this? I don't think so. If someone had asked me five years ago if this were possible, I would have said no. I felt it wasn't possible due to my underlying feelings of unworthiness. But now with my heart gradually opening up each day, the more I see, the more I believe.

I have seen visions before. I reflected back on them as I drove home from church tonight with Renee. One experience stands out in my mind. It happened one night as I put Mackenzie to bed. We finished a meditation together and this is what happened.

As I sat in awe, I said, "Mackenzie, your room just filled up with angels. See if you can see them." I didn't tell her that the room was full of gold. I wanted to know if she could really see the angels. I told her to look from her mind's eye, which comes from the center of your head and emanates out through the middle of your forehead.

Mackenzie said, "Mommy, I see them. The room is full of gold."

I was so excited! She could see them, and saw them in the same way I did. I was not only excited for her, but excited for me, too. She was validating me. I wanted to believe that the angels were here. I had felt their presence before, but to see them is unbelievable...so unbelievable that I have often questioned myself...until this experience happened.

I saw five angels in Mackenzie's room that night, but I didn't tell her this. Again, I wanted her to tell me what she saw. Then one moved across the room by her bed.

I asked her, "Mackenzie, how many do you see?"

"I see five, Mommy."

"I get there is one here who is your very special guardian angel. See if you can see where it is."

"It's right here by my bed, Mommy."

I couldn't believe this! That night was so special. I was thrilled, not only for my daughter, but for me, too. I remember thinking that I am not crazy for seeing these visions. I see other visions in my spiritual coaching sessions, but they are more based on people's past experiences and help me to clear out their emotional pain. The angel visions that I have seen, and now my daughter, too, are divine.

As I continued my drive home tonight, the thoughts

 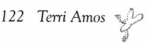

raced through my mind. I truly believe that I had a most blessed experience in church. I hesitated to share this with Renee, but as usual it came blurting from my mouth. I was shocked by her reaction.

Renee jumped up and down in her seat, giggling. "Oh, no, Terri. I can't believe this. I had the same thing happen tonight. Only I saw my dad instead of Jesus. I felt the angels, too. I'm not believing this!"

My heart tells me that Jesus was a "truth-seeker," an example of unconditional love, sent here by God for humans to see. Renee sees her father the same way. They are both gifts of love from above, and tonight we were blessed to see them. The joy that both Renee and I feel can't be described. We feel so much love and excitement. We have committed our lives to finding our truths and being led to the light. We've been on this journey for some time now.

When you fill your heart with the intent to heal and to find unconditional love, the miracles begin. For me they started out small. For instance, when I first started my coaching business I wanted a colorful brochure to match my business cards, but when I priced it, it was too expensive. At exercise class one day, my instructor remarked on how pretty the cards were. I told her I was disappointed at not being able to do my flyers in the same way. Out of the corner of the room came this man whom I had never met before. He started questioning me about the flyer and asked me what price I had been quoted to print it. I told him. Then he asked me if I had the flyer on a computer disc. I said yes and then he shocked me. He said "Give it to me."

"What do you mean?" I asked.

"Give it to me. I'll do it for you."

"How much is this going to cost me?" I expected the worst, although I figured it couldn't be nearly as bad as the last bid.

That one had been $1,000.

"I'll do it for free. I can't stand it when printing companies rip people off."

My mouth dropped. There had to be a catch. I wanted to get the flyers as soon as possible, because I wanted to send them out before Mother's Day.

"What is the turnaround time?"

Again, I expected the worst. He told me that he works for a huge printing company. I figured it would take him at least a month to get the flyers back to me.

"Three days," was his response. "I can get them to you in three days. Just give me the paper you want."

I knew in that moment that I was heading down the right path, finally, in my life. He was like an angel sent from above to help me on my way.

One last miracle that I want to share with you occurred when I had been working from my home for a while. I had thought about getting an office, but had not made any calls, nor inquired about it at all. It had been a simple thought. Then one day the phone rang. A girl I had met the year prior was calling. She is a massage therapist. She told me she was finding herself working more out of the office than in it and had decided to find someone to sublet the space. She said my name had come to her three different times and so, she said, she had to call to find out if I was interested in renting the space. Of course, I was, and a wonderful deal was struck.

With both of these miracles I began to see the work of God. I believe this is so because I opened my heart up to my truth and turned to trust. I believe whatever energy we give off attracts a similar energy from the universe. Like attracts like. If I have negative thoughts, then I attract negative situations. On the other hand, if I am in a space of love and trust, then the miracles begin.

I took baby steps moving into trust. But as those baby steps have matured and as I have matured within my spiritual journey, the miracles have grown. That's why where before I couldn't believe in seeing angels and the presence of God, now I do. And so can you, if you choose to open your heart to the truth and trust in the universe.

Thoughts for Your Journey

How does this journal entry make you feel? Do you find it hard to believe in miracles? Is it possible that you can't believe because you don't feel as if a miracle could ever happen to you? Go within and find your truth. Write your feelings.

When you feel that you can't believe in the beautiful messages from God, or if you believe in them but just can't imagine them happening to you, then it's probably because you don't feel worthy. Ask yourself if this rings true for you and then write down why you feel this way. Imagine pulling your child within up into your arms. Tell this little kid that he or she is completely worthy of all God's miracles and love.

Remember, you are worthy. We all are!

PATIENCE

Patience is a form of love that doesn't come easily, especially for me. I prayed for patience today. Then I was presented a beautiful gift.

I volunteer in Kolbi's class every other week. I help with reading. I do a one-on-one exercise with each student where they have to read a list of words. If they don't get a word, then that word goes on their word ring. It looks like a key chain. They keep this ring at their desks and practice the words when they can. Then the next time they see me or another volunteer they go over the words on the ring before starting a new list. If they can read a word, they get to rip it off the ring. It is a huge accomplishment to rip a word off. . .it's almost ceremonial for some of the kids.

Today, I was given a test. Of course, this came right after praying for patience. There is one little child in the class who has some learning disabilities. And if I am truly honest, I often try to avoid working with this child because it takes so much patience to get through the reading. Well, I had no choice today.

I will call this child Lee. Lee has a hard time sitting still and on average usually has at least twelve words left on the ring. Many of the students have none. Today was no exception for Lee. Because I was in the awareness of being patient, I began to focus on that. Every time Lee started fidgeting or looking up at the ceiling I said, "Lee, you have a choice. You can be here and focus, because I really want to work with you. Or you can choose not to work, but then I'll have to ask you to go back to your seat and let someone work with me who wants to." When Lee's focus meandered I stayed calm and came back to these words. And each time Lee came back to focusing. One by one, Lee laid out every word ripped from the ring. Before we knew it, the desk was covered with words; Lee had read all twelve of them. Wow! Neither one of us could believe it, nor could the teacher. Lee came away feeling on top of the world and I came away with a precious gift.

Working with Lee reminded me that patience comes from within. It is a choice. I have to get completely in the present moment and stay focused, just as Lee did, to be able to stay in that space. From being in that present moment I found that I am capable of a lot of patience. I let go of my fear that I couldn't work well with Lee. I let go of impatience, which is a huge task for me. But I did it and so did Lee. We are both still celebrating.

From this amazing gift I was also reminded to be patient with myself, and others, while on our journeys. Just like Lee, we all get it at some time or another. Everyone is different and where a large part of the kids in that first grade class may fly through their word rings with ease, there will always be some who won't. It doesn't matter. We all have issues to work out in this lifetime. For Lee it just happens to be through a learning disability. For me, well I've got quite a few. But the one thing I discovered today is that I can be patient if I choose.

Thoughts for Your Journey

When you think of the word "patience," what thoughts come to your mind? Do you feel guilty? Do you feel angry? Write about your feelings and any memories that surface for you.

Impatience is based in fear. When you find yourself impatient, ask what you are afraid of in that moment. Go into awareness with this and write down your discoveries.

You Are Worthy of Living Powerfully

I have been dealing with myself as a woman. Am I as deserving as a man? Yes. Yes, I am, but I am only now discovering that I am as worthy as a man.

For the last week "men" have come up in my talks with friends. Patty and I were walking one day and I was telling her how I hate it when men tell me I am pretty. "What about the inside of me, you jerk? Why don't you ask me what is going on in my life?" The anger exploded out of me as I relayed to Patty what went through my mind when men demeaned me. Or at least when I felt their words demeaned me. Patty backed up. She could feel the intensity of what I was saying. Even I was surprised. I guess I was moving deeper into a new healing space and hadn't realized it. Deep-seated anger was surfacing that I didn't know existed.

This issue has been unfolding in front of my eyes for years. There was a time when my husband would walk into the house and I would shut down. I blamed him for taking away my power. He wasn't. I figured this out eventually, but it almost ruined our marriage in the process. I was transferring my issues with my dad onto Steve. I shut down for fear that if I spoke up, Steve would reject me. It was about that dad authoritative energy and being fearful of not receiving acceptance and love from it.

As I began to heal my life and take responsibility for it, I took the blame away from Steve and my dad. It was the best thing I ever did. Steve and I have a wonderful marriage now. It has taken some work, though.

Last year on Fourth of July, for instance, came a mile

marker for discovering my self-worth. Mackenzie really wanted to go to a friend's party. Steve kept saying "no." He didn't want to go, so therefore, none of us were going. She hounded us for at least two hours. I found myself saying, "Mackenzie, your dad doesn't want to go. We are not going." This didn't feel right to me. I felt as if I were betraying myself. I got into the shower and meditated. I found my truth.

"Mackenzie, your feelings are every bit as important as your father's. I'm sorry we've made his out to be more important. There is no reason why you can't go to that party." When I told her this I got a big hug and a kiss.

"Mom, I don't think I want to go anymore. I want to stay home with the family." Mackenzie's feelings had been acknowledged, she shifted and so did I.

In my family, growing up, everything centered on my dad. He was the protector and the provider. His word was like God's word and he definitely had the last say. I was treating Steve the same with our kids. When I discussed this with Steve, however, he enlightened me. He said that he didn't feel it was just about little girls. He said that as a little boy he felt the same way about his father and that it still lingered with him.

That's when I thought I was done with this issue. I thought I finally had an understanding, until just recently. That's when all of these "less than" feelings started bubbling up again. I want to be as powerful as men. I have a right to. I want to be treated with the same respect as men. I want to be valued for what is on the inside, rather than what is on the outside. I don't want to feel that their word is the last word.

Then something profound happened during meditation at church the other night. I heard, "Terri, your anger is not with men. It is with yourself." During the rest of the service the puzzle came together.

I am as powerful as men. I am the one holding me back.

I didn't feel I was good enough to get the same respect. I didn't feel I was valued. My father was the one valued in our household. I wasn't. I am the one who continues to buy into this picture. It is a societal one. . .one that says men have the authority...one that has been handed down from the beginning of time. I realize that this chain has been in the process of being broken for quite some time. I am the one who holds onto the link that keeps the chain intact in my life. No one is the authority in my life. I am, with God as my guide.

It is up to me to remember that I am worthy of the same kind of power that I have given to men all of my life. It's not about men. It's about me. It's remembering that we are all equal. . .all divine beings worthy of living powerfully.

Thoughts for Your Journey

When you read this journal entry, what feelings surface about people in authority?

Watch your interactions with others today and notice when you value others more than yourself. Are you handing your power over to someone you feel has more authority? Why do you not trust yourself? What do you find out about yourself?

ALLOW YOURSELF TO BE LOVED

It is four o'clock in the morning. The light casts a shadow of warmth in the room. My rocking chair goes back and forth, back and forth. My baby nurses at my breast. Everything is so quiet. . .so still. This is our sacred space. This is where we feel so connected, so at one with each other. Nothing comes between us. There is no fear. There is only love.

These are my memories of my babies. I yearn for this feeling again. Only this time I yearn to be the baby cradled in my mother's warm enveloping embrace. I yearn to feel completely loved.

I realize that I haven't allowed myself to feel so loved. I am the one who does the nurturing. . .with my children, my family and friends. I don't allow myself to go to that place of vulnerability. I am in fear. I have built my whole life on looking so strong. . .so powerful. I haven't allowed myself to open up to feel the love. I feared I would not be worthy. I feared I would be rejected. I feared I would appear weak. I feared I would be judged.

"God help me to let go of these fears. I am worthy of love. I know this. Now help me to own this. Help me to feel this love in every cell of my body. Please show me the way. I am putting my pride and my power into your hands. I am crawling up into your arms of light feeling the warmth of your loving embrace. Tears are flowing down my face. I weep, for I have arrived. Please, God, let me stay in this sacred space. Show me the way to allow myself to bring this love into every moment of my life in every breath that I take. . .for I know I am the one who keeps the love away."

Thoughts for Your Journey

Are you holding love at bay? What are you afraid of?

Go into your meditation garden again. Ask for God's presence to surround you. Let your fear slide away. Feel the warmth of God's embrace. Write your discoveries.

WHOSE APPROVAL ARE YOU SEEKING?

I'm not going "crazy." Yeah! This is the time of year when life begins to feel like an avalanche. It is when I usually get so overwhelmed that I feel smothered and out of control. It is normally when I get the angriest. . .but not this year.

I am celebrating this awareness. This is what I call the "end of the school year madness." Starting from May 20th to June 20th, all three of our kids have their birthdays. Then add Mother's Day, Memorial Day and Father's Day to the list. Include school parties, school talent shows, school band recitals, dance recitals, school open house and on and on. I'm not even listing all of the rehearsals and normal stuff that go along with this craziness. Just reading this could make a person panic. But I'm not panicking. Finally.

I used to be so caught up in how perfect everything looked and how others might perceive my efforts when it came to the parties. "Am I doing it well enough?" or "Will they think my kid's party was fun?" These were questions I pondered in my head. Because I was so caught up in these judgment pictures, I got angry. Everything became an effort and everyone, in my mind, was to blame. I found myself screaming, crying and pointing fingers at anyone who was in my way. Everyone felt bad. Of course, the parties always came off without a hitch, but then I felt blue afterwards. I felt blue for the guilt of hurting my family along the way and because I was not following my truth. I was looking for approval from the outside, rather than from within.

All that has changed now. Since I've decided to forgive myself and ease up on those perfect pictures I had, life is running a lot smoother. Now don't get me wrong, I do have my "moments" still. But when I do, I catch myself. I know enough now to not stay in blame with those around me. I'll stop, see what I am in fear of, breathe, and make some time for myself. The more I love myself, the more I am able to love what I am doing for others.

This crazy time is a wonderful opportunity for healing. Just being aware of when I do go into that fear mode is key. For instance, Mackenzie was in the school talent show the other night. Butterflies bombed my stomach. "Why am I nervous?" I asked myself. "That's not me up there performing."

Pictures flashed through my mind of when I was a kid performing. I saw the good times and the ones that were not so good. . .like when I forgot my lines in a play or when I forgot certain dance steps in a recital or parade. I saw how I was putting my fears on Mackenzie. "This is her life, not yours, Terri. Relax, sit back and enjoy," I reassured myself.

As I watched the pictures of my life flash before me, I was able to ask myself what was going on in each one of them. My answer was that I was seeking approval. Just as I used to be with my kids' birthday parties, I wanted people to like me and to think I was doing a job well. Just by being aware of this, I found peace. I have approval now. It is within my heart. And as far as Mackenzie is concerned, she'll have to discover hers for herself. She is on her own journey. . .a time for her to recognize her spirit and the love within. Allowing Mackenzie to live her own life is the best gift I can give her. . .letting her experience the joys and pains of life and discovering her truth amongst all of it.

Thoughts for Your Journey

How are you dealing with your life right now? Are you beating yourself up trying to be "good enough?" Whose approval are you seeking? What are you afraid of here?

The fact that you are taking the time to read this book and answer these questions gives cause for celebration. When was the last time you patted yourself on the back and said "Nicely done?" Remember, it's really up to you to give yourself approval! Find some way to celebrate and write about it.

GUILT IS DEBILITATING

It is two o'clock in the morning. I'm not sure why, but I can't sleep. As I roam around the house, I find myself looking at a picture on the fireplace mantel. It is filled with God's grace. . .two little angels sent from heaven above, holding hands, dressed in pink, pure with innocence. They are my girls, God's gift to me.

I weep with regret. What have I done to them? How has my anger and pride affected them? I am buried in guilt.

"Oh, God, please give me peace with this. I love them so much. They are your light in the purest sense. Please don't let it be too late. I am human. I make mistakes. Please let them forgive me. I pray I've caused them no pain."

And then I sleep.

As I awaken this morning I hear, "Guilt and regrets are just reminders, Terri. Forgive yourself."

My goal in this lifetime is to love unconditionally. As I continue along this path, I have to constantly forgive myself. I know guilt is debilitating. It creates walls. . .walls of anger and resentment. . . walls of false pride. It is a fear of being judged for mistakes been made. I know this. It is okay. I also know that I have spiritual agreements with each of the people in my life. We are here to learn from one another. I believe this is true.

As I remind myself of this, the guilt begins to subside. The little child inside of me is human. To be human is to make mistakes. I've made quite a few.

For many years I carried a lot of guilt because of my relationship with A.J. I was extremely hard on him. That's because I was hard on myself. I didn't know any other way. I felt caged. Pain and anger ran rampant within our home. I was in severe frustration. I remember screaming and yelling at him and then sobbing with guilt and regret. I didn't know how to turn off the pain. Then the gift came.

Steve, A.J., Donna (A.J.'s mom) and I got into therapy. It was an avenue for us all to look at ourselves. It was the beginning stages of letting go of the blame. Through understanding we started to release the pain.

Now I can honestly say that I am thankful for all that we went through. I don't feel guilt with A.J. anymore...there is only gratitude, at least most of the time. That dark period was a catalyst for me to turn to God's light.

Because I've chosen to let go of the guilt of my past, I've learned about loving myself and finding compassion for my humanness, as well as others'. And even though I still struggle with guilt sometimes, I find that when I look back on the angry times and on the sad times, there is always a gift. That gift is love...a gift to discover who I am. And isn't that what it's all about, to remember who we are? Therefore, there is no room for guilt. There is only room for gratitude...gratitude for finally remembering that we each are the light. We go through the darkness to discover the light. It's so beautiful!

Thoughts for Your Journey

Is there guilt lingering in your life? What do you feel guilty about?

Close your eyes and feel the pain of the guilt you are holding onto. Let it drain away. Let the tension ease from your mind. See the situation you feel guilty about. What is the gift here? Even in the worst of situations there is something to learn. This is your time to heal. Write about your findings.

VULNERABILITY IS AN ACT OF COURAGE

My heart is filled with tears like the ocean's tides, ebbing and flowing, never quite knowing when they are coming or going. Some are tears of sadness and some are tears of joy. The point is that they are coming. I am finally letting go.

My whole life I thought that to cry was to be weak. . .to be vulnerable. I remember watching my mom and sister cuddling on the couch across the room from me. They sat there crying about some sad movie. I didn't allow myself to weep. I separated myself. My heart wanted to be a part of their circle of love, but my mind said no. If I joined in, it meant that I had given in. I would have to be like them. Why was I afraid? I really don't know, other than I heard my dad's remarks about how important it was to be strong. As a result, I disowned my femininity. I lost sight of the little girl within me and shut down my vulnerability.

Now, as I'm finally letting down my walls, I discover that to show vulnerability is not to be weak, but it is to be strong, for what courage it takes to open up your heart to the pain. I am courageous! I never thought of myself this way, but now I do. I faced my pain with determination and drive that I never knew I had. I am so proud of myself.

My tears may make it seem as if I'm constantly sad, but don't be fooled. My husband was today. "Terri, sometimes things make us sad. You just have to push by it."

"Steve, I don't want to push by this. I want it to flow. Yes, there is sadness inside of me. It's been there for years. There are many tears because I've held so much in over the years. I don't want to stuff the tears in anymore. I know that if I let them flow and they go, then there will be peace. I know in my heart that people are sick and angry because they don't let themselves feel the pain. I don't want to be in pain anymore."

So I cried the rest of this day. . .sometimes in joy, sometimes in pain. As a result, this poem came.

I have felt so alone
For many a day
Hiding behind a facade
Strength was the play
I saw emotions as weak
Vulnerability to be shamed
A wall built so strong
I was in denial of the pain

Why I chose this route
I can't surely say
I bought into my dad's life
It was the tougher way
He saw my mother as weak
Her tears were a strain
They reminded him of his failure
He couldn't ease her pain

So in the end I became tough
On the outside at least
But within filled with anger
Some would call it the "Beast"
Anger took over my life
Battling it was a game
Until the day I lost my dad
Since then, I've never been the same

I chose a path of healing
This wicked demon of mine
What I've found is a love within
It feels so much more divine
But as the love grows ever stronger
And my walls begin to fail
The tears begin to ebb and flow
Like the winds in a sail

Some are tears of sadness
Some are tears of pain
Some are tears of joy
For peace has been gained
My heart is fully opened
My mind is at rest
Life is flowing through me
I feel so truly blessed

Thoughts for Your Journey

Are you holding your emotions inside? What does this journal entry reflect in your life?

Allow yourself to "feel" whatever is going on in your life right now. Allowing this is true acceptance. By not stuffing your pain inside you or pushing it away, you are saying that it is "okay." This is giving yourself permission to be human. Write your discoveries.

BELIEVE IN YOURSELF

It is the last softball game of the year. Kolbi is up to bat. She looks scared, unsure. Strike one, strike two, strike three, she's out. I feel sick to my stomach.

Why is this making me anxious? I know this is not about Kolbi. I see myself as a kid. I played many sports, softball, basketball, volleyball, and even football in my backyard and in college. What is my spirit trying to show me?

I flash back on all of the times when coaches were giving me a good talking to. I felt so inadequate. I thought they were reprimanding me. But as I am watching Kolbi, much like her, I realize that I was the one holding me back. They all saw the potential in me. I was the one who didn't believe.

I ask myself why I held myself back. "I was in fear" is the answer I receive. I didn't believe I was good enough.

I see how that picture has stayed with me my whole life. I never really thought that I was good enough to have success in my life. I didn't feel I was worthy. Of course, I didn't think of it in those terms. I just convinced myself that I was doing the best that I could. And maybe I was. I didn't know any better.

I do know better now, and yet I have continued to buy into those debilitating pictures. I have understood for a long time that I am worthy. . .that God loves me and that I am acceptable. However, I have just really begun to "own" it. There is a difference. It is like the old saying, "You can talk the talk, but can you walk the walk?" Well, I had the knowledge; I just hadn't integrated it into every cell of my body. I have begun that process now and it feels so very good.

On the other hand, if I now recognize that I am worthy

and am starting to own it, then why am I being "lit up" by Kolbi on the softball field? I ask myself this question. The answer doesn't come quickly.

It is now two days later. I've been shooting hoops over the past few days for exercise. I am amazed at how the ball flows from my hands. I don't remember feeling this way when I played ball in school. The ball swooshes through the hoop and with that two-pointer I know my truth.

I "believe" I can do it. I know I can make those hoops. I know I am good enough. That is the difference now. Not only am I worthy of playing well, but also, I believe I am good enough. I believe it and, therefore, it is.

Feeling worthy comes from believing that all people are equal and that we are all capable of living powerfully. It is believing that each of us has the potential to do great things.

Feeling "good enough," on the other hand, is a belief in myself that I can live up to that potential. I believe that I am worthy. The question I pose to myself is: "Am I good enough to live in all of my possibilities?" Well, if I am made to be worthy of living powerfully, then the only person or thing that is holding me back from it is me. It is my fear.

Now as I live my daily life as a wife and mom, as a spiritual coach, as a teacher and a writer, I believe it's up to me to live in all of my possibilities. I am worthy. Now it is up to me to trust in the power that I know is within me. No one is holding me back. . .especially not me. . .not anymore. I choose to believe!

Thoughts for Your Journey

Are you living in all of your possibilities? What is it that keeps you holding yourself back? What are you afraid of when facing this?

Remember, you are the only one who can hold you back. Write down what your life would look like right now if you chose to let go and live in all of your possibilities.

Learn to Laugh at Yourself

Life keeps smacking me square in the face. I asked for healing and, boy, am I getting it. I feel like an onion. Each layer gets peeled away to uncover past pain. I welcome it, because I know that as soon as I allow it to surface, only then can it fall away.

My girls are always at the forefront of my healing. As I've said so many times before, they are the reflections to my soul. Today, Mackenzie gave me another lesson.

We have a teacher at our elementary school who loves to line dance. He invites the third graders to learn a series of line dances at recess. He starts the whole process at the beginning of the year and it culminates with a big recital. Well, this morning was the big show.

Mackenzie loves to dance and has a great gift for it. She has been rehearsing all year, but I never saw any of it because it was to be a surprise. It was and it was fabulous. She was even a line leader and did beautifully.

I, on the other hand, was vibrating like an old coin-operated hotel bed. As I sat there with a knot in my stomach, I had to ask, "Why?" The answer I got was "humiliation." As I watched Mackenzie dance I felt the old fears of being embarrassed. Most of us have probably felt that way sometime in our lives. I just didn't know this was still lingering with me. Obviously, I don't want my child to embarrass herself. I don't want her to feel the pain that I did, that pain of humiliation, the pain of not performing to that perfect picture I had set for myself.

Then I realize that this is exactly what this is, a perfect picture again. I reflect back on my life and an old teacher comes to mind. His name is Mr. Nash and he was my eleventh grade history teacher. Mr. Nash gave me one of the best gifts of my life. . .he told me I needed to learn to laugh at myself. He planted one of the seeds that allowed me to change my life. I have been laughing at myself ever since.

And now I get to laugh at myself again. So what if my daughter messes up. Yes, it might be painful and it might not be. That's for her to decide. It's her life. All I can do is love her, support her and allow her to be on her own journey.

As for me, I can see that with each time there has been humiliation in my life it has helped me along my way. When I was younger, I beat myself up from embarrassment and always found others to blame. Then over time I began to laugh on the outside at embarrassing times, but still cry on the inside and hold onto the pain. Eventually, the crying died completely, but the fear has stayed with me. . .until today.

I don't have to have this fear in my life anymore. So what if I humiliate myself again? I trust myself enough now to know that it's not who I am. It's just a moment in time that means nothing. Embarrassment and humiliation are just judgments we put on ourselves for feeling a lack of who we think we "should" be. I understand that I am who I am. . .mistakes and all. . .and that's okay with me.

Thoughts for Your Journey

What humiliating memories come back to you after reading this entry? What was the gift from each of these situations?

Does the fear of embarrassment hold you back? What is the worst that could happen to you?

When you learn to laugh at yourself during humiliating times, you give others permission to laugh at themselves, too.

NURTURE THE PAIN

"Kolbi, are you feeling okay?" I have finally found a moment of compassion for Kolbi. She's resisting everything lately, especially me.

It is the last full week of the school year and she is burned out. She's only in the first grade and is loaded down with homework and a book report. She has no desire to put any effort into it and I feel like an ogre for staying on top of her about it. I am burned out, too. This is too much responsibility for a six-year-old. And, quite honestly, it's too much for me, too.

"Mommy, I feel so bad." Kolbi climbs up onto my lap sobbing. I want to sob, too. She's going through a hard time right now. It's another transition time, a growth period. And what have I done? I've added to her pain and frustration because of my own. What we both need is to be nurtured.

As I hold her and rock her back and forth, life starts to flash by. What are we doing to our children and those around us? What are we doing to ourselves? The times we are most resistant and stuck are when we really need to be nurtured. We don't need to beat ourselves up. We need to love ourselves.

I realize that Kolbi just needs to be loved right now in spite of her resistance. Resistance is just fear. She doesn't deserve to be beaten up emotionally because of her fear. She deserves to be loved and nurtured so she can find her way through this hard time. . .so she can find her truth. . .just like me. . .just like you.

"God, help me to honor myself, and others, in the good and the bad times. Love and compassion are the keys. Please fill my heart with these. Please give me a gentle heart and a gentle tongue. Show me the way to send love to the pain."

Thoughts for Your Journey

The little child within you needs to be nurtured to feel loved. Close your eyes. See your child within and ask what he or she needs right now. Write down your discoveries.

Try to speak to the little child within as many times today as you can. It only takes a moment to do this. Keep this in your awareness today. At the end of the day, check in with yourself. How do you feel? Could you follow through with what the child needed from you? If so, congratulations for listening and taking action. If you struggled with this, ask God to help you send love to your pain and see the gift of this situation.

You Can Have Abundance

My husband is known for his "Midas touch." Almost everything he touches turns to gold.

We are in Las Vegas. He's here on business. I'm here for a day away. The blackjack table was calling his name last night. "Just for a little fun," he said. Well, two hours later I had blown through his hard-earned money. . .$200 of it. . .and I felt terrible.

Steve has been to Vegas twice in the last month on business. He came home both times as a winner from "having a little fun" at the tables. He's not a gambler. He's just lucky. His luck comes from a positive attitude. . .and knowing when to quit, of course!

"Terri, you have to let go of this issue about money. It brings negative vibes."

He's right. I've been lucky with money, but with limits. I have never wanted for anything because I didn't allow myself to. A lot has been provided to me from my husband, old boyfriends and my family. But I never allowed myself complete financial abundance. I haven't allowed myself to receive this kind of love from the universe. Like everything else in my life, I put the boundaries on myself. With success, with havingness, with love, I put limits. Therefore, I put limits on how I spend my husband's hard-earned money. Losing it doesn't feel good.

I believe I set these limits on myself because my parents did the same. From their example, I learned you don't give money to yourself. You give it to those you love. They gave everything they had to my sister and me. As a child, I saw that it was selfish to take money as an adult, especially from your loved ones. Ironically, I saw my parents lose everything in bankruptcy. Now, because of what I've learned on my spiritual journey, I believe this was a reflection of their inner programming. I believe the universe gave them what they thought about themselves. Their programming said they couldn't have financial abundance, so they didn't.

"Honey, why do you think you've been so successful financially? Is it because you felt you had to prove yourself to others?" We are at dinner and I am picking Steve's brain. I want to know what makes him seem so successful and, as a result, financially abundant.

"Well, it used to be some of that," Steve responds, "wanting to prove others wrong. But the real driving force is I have always asked myself, 'Why can't I?' I never find an answer that tells me I can't have what I want."

I realize his answer is the key to living powerfully in all areas of life, not just with success and financial abundance. Steve doesn't put limits on himself, at least not with these parts of his life. He knows there is no one holding him back except himself. And with that he dreams big, he thinks positively. . .he creates financial freedom for himself. He has no boundaries when it comes to success and creating financial abundance.

Once again, I see that I am the one who has put the limits on myself my whole life. Why can't I do anything, be anything, be everything I want to be? Why can't I give to myself and live abundantly? There is no answer other than "I can." I am the answer through thinking positively, believing in myself, and letting go of the boundaries. And by giving myself permission to live abundantly, I break the cycle and set the example for my kids to live abundantly, as well. All things are possible if I just believe. It's like my favorite childhood book, *The Little Engine That Could*, "I think I can, I think I can." I know I can!

Thoughts for Your Journey

Are you stuck in the "I can'ts?" Why can't you have financial abundance? What thoughts or feelings arise after reading this journal entry?

As we peel away the layers of the onion that surround us, we discover limits on ourselves that we hadn't recognized until now. What limits have you discovered lately? What ones are you ready to release? Start checking in to see when you are limiting yourself.

ALLOW GOD TO USE YOU

I ask God to use me each and every day. Today, God did.

My friend, Renee, is a wonderful singer. She hasn't fully claimed her gift. She knows it's there, but like me, tends to hold herself back. She has a wonderful opportunity right now to work with a record producer. And, yet, she's stuck in the "I can'ts."

I was reminded of my purpose today when visiting with Renee on the phone. It would have been very easy for the old me to get caught up in my ego and feel jealous of this opportunity before her. Instead, I found God using me. It feels so good. I helped Renee to discover her power and to let go of her old guilt pictures. . .pictures that were keeping her stuck.

I didn't realize what I had done until just now sitting in my car listening to a beautiful song by Rickie Byars called *Use Me* from the CD, *I Found a Deeper Love*. The song says, "Command my hands, what must they do? Command my life, it's here for you." Now as I weep with joy, I realize I am living powerfully. I am able to step away from my ego and allow God's essence to flow through me. I am able to be "unconditional love." By coming from a space of love to help others live more powerfully, I am, in return, powerful.

I am overwhelmed by this gift that God has shown me. I feel so much gratitude for Renee and the spirit that she is and for allowing me to find my truth. I am powerful. . . I am spirit...I am the essence of love!

Thoughts for Your Journey

We live more powerfully by helping others to discover their power. Go into an awareness of allowing the spirit to flow through you, rather than the ego. Ask God to help you with this. See if you can find a way to help someone live powerfully today without giving up yourself. Write your discoveries.

After being in this awareness today, did you have a hard time allowing the spirit to flow through you? If you did, ask what fears are allowing the ego to control your life.

TRUST IN GOD'S PLAN

I was stood up yesterday. . .not just by one person. . .but by a whole class! What a gift this was for me.

I had been asked to teach a workshop at a yoga studio. I held one there last month and it went great. So when the owner of the studio asked me to come back and hold a class that was to have been yesterday, my ego said I had to do it. My heart on the other hand said, "This is not such a good idea, Terri. This is your kids' dance recital weekend and it's Father's Day weekend. How are you going to fit it all in?"

Well, my ego won out. I didn't listen to my truth and went ahead and planned the class. And then wouldn't you know it. . .no one showed up. I actually laughed with relief when I arrived and there wasn't anyone there but the owners and me.

So now, as I look at this, I see I was in fear. I didn't believe that if I put the owners off for a month or so that they would still want me to teach. I wasn't in trust with God's plan. My ego was in control. And as a result, I was shown that when I work from a place of fear and try to control things, life doesn't necessarily tend to go as we hope or plan.

This is how the ego plays with us. It puts us into fear. It gets us all confused to the point where we don't know our truth. That's what it did with me when I had to make a choice on whether or not to teach that class. My ego got in the way, so I didn't believe in myself enough to trust in God's plan.

Now I know I must work from a space of being in my truth, for I know that when I am in my truth, I am working with God. The light is coming through. I just have to be willing to listen for the guidance and trust that it is the plan.

Thoughts for Your Journey

The ego is that part of you that keeps you in fear. Watch yourself today and be aware of when your ego and spirit are having a battle of wills. Write your discoveries.

Acknowledge the ego. Try to be in acceptance of it. After all, you are a spirit first that came in to learn from it. This is your humanness. Be with your fears and allow them to move through you. If any pain arose for you after today's awareness, this is good. Feel it. Let it bubble up from deep down within you. Write your thoughts and feelings about this.

ARE YOU TO BLAME?

It was a beautiful day today. . .in more ways than one. The sky was blue, the smell of summer was at hand and celebrations began for the end of the school year. Mackenzie's class had a big picnic at the park to close out her third grade year.

I went to check out what was going on, to see the kids having some fun. I gave Mackenzie a big hug and asked her if she was still mad at me. She was blaming me for everything wrong in her life earlier this morning. I knew she was just tired and burned out from a long year.

"No," was her response with a big hug in return and then she ran off giggling.

A woman was standing beside me watching our little encounter. As Mackenzie ran off, I turned to the lady laughing and said, "Oh, she's always mad at me about something."

The lady's response was this, "It ruins my whole day when my kids are mad at me."

I could relate. That's how it's been my whole life as a mom. Every time my kids and I fought or just struggled, I took it personally. . .but not anymore. Of course, I have my moments and sometimes I have complete days of darkness, but overall, I'm finally starting to integrate some of the information I've been learning. I don't have to get caught up in my kids' stories. Just because one of them might be having a bad day doesn't mean I am always to blame. I'm finally starting to discern when I'm being a pain in the rump. There have been many times in the past when I took the blame when my kids were in pain and it wasn't my fault.

This scenario has happened, not only with my kids, but

with my husband, too. I can't tell you how many times he has come in from a hard day of work and I have shut down. If he was in a sour mood, then I felt I had to be, too. This doesn't do anyone any good.

I'm finally starting to understand that if I can remember my truth and live in it, rather than in other people's stories, my life runs a lot smoother. I am a lot happier and I can be a support for others during their pain. I just have to be willing to ask, "Am I to blame?" If I go within and find that I am the cause, then I need to look at what's hurting inside of me. I have to own the responsibility. On the other hand, if I know in my heart that this is another person's story, then I can set myself free and allow them to "be."

Thoughts for Your Journey

Do you still "own" all of the blame for other people's pain? Or are you beginning to stay out of their stories? Write your feelings.

Take a look at how much information you have begun to integrate in your life. It's time to pat yourself on the back again. Are you doing this enough? Write down what you are thankful for learning during this leg of you journey. How has your life changed?

YOU DESERVE RESPECT

If you want people to respect you, you must first respect yourself.

I don't know where I lost respect for myself along the way. Maybe it was when I was somewhere around the age of 15 and a modeling agent molested me. I let him touch my breasts because I thought that was what I had to do to be accepted. But when I think about this, I realize I must have lost my self-respect sometime before that or else I wouldn't have let him violate me. Why did I allow this man to touch me? I'm not sure. I just know that this is very painful to write about. I thought I was done with this. This surfaced in my memory a couple of years ago. I had buried it so very deeply. And then it started erupting from deep within my soul.

I thought the culmination of the pain from this molestation came when I was in Cabo San Lucas a few years back. I was dancing, doing the Macarena, with a bunch of friends. My friend, Lisa, was letting her hair down. She was going around flipping up her top on the dance floor and acting as if she was going to do it to others, as well. She had been doing this for the past few days every time we went dancing. I warned her earlier in the day not to do it to me. All of the pain of my molestation was surfacing. Well, what did she go and do? She flipped up my dress as a joke. It was no joke to me and I hit her. I know this wasn't the loving thing to do, but I couldn't help it. I felt no love. I felt only pain. I was humiliated. I felt so violated. The funny thing about it is that for a few moments I tried to make everything better with her. I tried to brush it off and make it like it was no big deal. I didn't hit her very hard. It was on her arm and it was more like what kids call a frog, so I said I had forgiven her and would she please forgive me. She was furious and couldn't at that time.

What was really going on was that I was trying to suppress my pain again and wasn't respecting myself. I was more worried about having Lisa's acceptance than I was about loving myself.

Steve dragged me back to our room and I cried for hours. I thought I had finally released the pain. That is, until now.

In the last month this has been resurfacing. I've gone deeper within. I was flooded with emotions recently when I told my husband that I had met a writer and that we were going to exchange works. We wanted to see what we could learn from each other. My husband's remark was, "Oh, he just wants to get into your pants."

I wanted to strangle him! Why would he say something like this? And when I told A.J. about the writer, he said the same thing. In my heart, I know they meant it as a joke and I know they thought they were paying me a compliment, but I deserve better than this. I understand that they would say this kind of remark to me because I didn't demand more respect for myself. I didn't treat myself with enough respect, so why should they? They were only following my lead.

This brings me to today. A.J. and I were in a conversation and the next thing I knew, he made a joke about my work. That did it. Just because it doesn't fit into the norm of what everyone else does, doesn't mean it is not worth respecting.

I know these situations have been a gift. I am so thankful, for I know they have shown me once again what I need to do for myself. I have to respect me. If I want to be respected, I must first respect myself. I cannot give myself up just to gain acceptance. It starts with me. I have to create my boundaries of what feels right. No one can do it for me; it has to come from within me.

Gradually, I get better with setting boundaries. Respect and boundaries not only pertain to what people say to me, but also, in how I allow them to act with me. For instance, as I've written this book, it has been up to me to draw the boundaries with my kids. I write in my home. I try not to do it when they are here, but there are times when I just can't help myself. As a result, I have had to let them know what my boundaries are. There are times I need solitude and so I ask them to leave. I have learned a huge lesson from all of this.

I deserve respect and I deserve the right to put up some boundaries. What I do is important to me. And even if no one else can accept me or respect me, I have to respect myself. This is one more giant step to wholeness.

Thoughts for Your Journey

After reading this entry, what feelings about boundaries and respect surface for you?

What can you do, beginning today, to respect yourself more? What boundaries can you create?

ACT UPON THE MESSAGES

Are you listening to that little voice within? This is God's voice trying to get a message to you.

I can't tell you how many times someone has come to me for a spiritual coaching session and said, when we were done, "Well, that's what I kept hearing for myself."

For example, a lady named Chris came in today. She has been stuck for a very long time in self-denial. She's been way too responsible for others and hasn't taken care of herself. Chris had forgotten or never knew how to be a little girl, because, as a child, she had to take care of everyone else. Throughout the session, the message was clear. Chris needs to honor the little girl inside herself.

As we finished, Chris told me she's asked for God's guidance and has received an answer many times. The message consistently says she needs to allow herself to be a little girl. . .and yet, she hasn't heeded God's advice. That is why she continues to be stuck. Chris needs to act upon what she is hearing.

This is what I call co-creating. . .to ask for God's guidance, listen for the answer, and then to act upon it.

I ask for my heart to be open every day to the divine will of God. Sometimes the answers come immediately, other times they seem far away. It's up to me to watch for a sign or to listen for a message. Then I can choose to act upon it. When I do, things come easily.

For instance, I recently decided to throw my husband a 50th birthday party. It is a spur-of-the-moment event and I needed to get the invitations out quickly. This is not my typical backyard barbeque. This is the "Big One" for Steve. So I asked all of my friends where to get the invites done quickly. I had no fewer than ten answers.

I followed the first suggestion and came to a dead end. As I sat in the mall parking lot, I said, "Okay, God, I could be doing this for days, searching for a place to do quick invites. However, that would defeat the purpose. I need your help."

Immediately I got my answer. Now it wasn't the closest place to go, but I decided to follow my guidance. I drove to the store, had the invitation picked out, designed and ready to be printed within an hour. I couldn't believe it! They were ready to be mailed within 24 hours. Just by listening and then acting upon the guidance, my life flowed a lot easier.

I believe this is a huge part of living powerfully. We must act on what our inner voice tells us. This is God speaking to us. We have to trust that it is real.

Like Chris, so many of us stay stuck in our lives even after receiving an answer. We are fearful to follow the advice. But what I have found is that as I've taken tiny little steps to trust the messages, then listening for the answers starts becoming an everyday occurrence in almost every situation. . .even for the little requests like something as trivial as making a party invitation. The result is a peaceful flow. By listening and acting upon it, there is no need for fear and control.

Thoughts for Your Journey

What keeps you from listening and acting upon the messages? What are you afraid of when it comes to following your guidance?

Spend some time going within. Ask for guidance on whatever you are concerned about. Believe what you hear and then act upon it. This is one giant step to turning your life over to trust. What do you discover?

HONOR YOUR NEED FOR CREATIVITY

It's time to check in. I feel a pressure on my chest and throat that feels somewhat like anxiety. I'm even having a hard time writing this. I feel I could throw up. "Why? Why, God, do I feel so disconnected right now?"

I think I know the answer. For the past month I have forgotten me. There has been so much going on with summer now in full bloom that I have once again forgotten myself.

What happened? I was doing so well. Somehow I lost touch. When I honor me creatively, I feel so fulfilled. That's because I am using my gifts. But now my writing has gone by the wayside, except for spurts here and there. It is where I allow myself to express fully. It is where I let my hair loose. It is where I allow my walls to come crumbling down.

I have to express myself creatively. We all do. We are all the essence of God's creativity. We are made in God's likeness, so therefore to be fully who we are, we must create. It is why we are here. But like most people, I have forgotten this of late.

I haven't written in weeks. I put myself on the backburner. I put my need to express behind everything else in my life. And now, I feel like I'm choking.

"Please, God, guide me to the light!"

Thoughts for Your Journey

How do you like to express yourself creatively? Are you allowing yourself some creative time? What feelings surface after reading this?

Find some way today to express yourself creatively. You can try anything your heart desires. There are many possibilities, such as writing, drawing, dancing, nature walking, or playing. Being creative is anything that you can perceive that makes you feel both happy and free. What are your discoveries?

You Are Extraordinary

To be ordinary is to be extraordinary. I remembered that just recently. I asked myself why our world seems to value ordinary people less than the extraordinary ones. I meditated on this and saw that it is the ego that confuses us. The answer is that there is no difference.

Whether you are a teacher, a wife, a company CEO, or a football pro, we are all the same. We make up the whole.

It takes each and every one of us to make up the whole. Everyone is needed to learn and heal from. After all, we are the mirrors to one another's souls.

You can be a simple housewife, if there is such a thing, and make a difference in people's lives. Just by the words you say or don't say. . .just by listening. . .through relationships, you heal the pain.

I wrote about a child named Lee earlier in my journey. Lee has learning disabilities and, yet, this child was a great gift to me. Lee taught me about patience and understanding.

In the beginning of this book, I also shared what I learned by seeing a homeless man lost in his fears. He was a magnificent gift to see. . .no less extraordinary than you or me.

It's all about healing. It's all about remembering our spirits. That's why we move in and out of time and place. We change. We grow. And where one day we might be the one who seems to be on top of the world, the next we might be lost in the valley so low. In those moments, to the human eye, the extraordinary becomes ordinary. It's not whether you are up or down; it's not whether you are slow or bright. What matters is for you to remember that you are already extraordinary. . .you are a spirit first, a part of God's light.

Thoughts for Your Journey

How do you see yourself? Are you extraordinary, ordinary, or somewhere in between? Write your feelings.

It's time for you to discover the extraordinary you! List why you are of value to the world around you.

IT'S TIME TO PLAY!

Boom! The waves pound around me. I attempt to ride them in search of my sanity. I have taken to the beautiful blue water of the Pacific with my kids. It is a gorgeous day with barely a breeze. Each ride on my boogie board carries me back to sanity. I become more alive. I am childlike with playfulness.

I am usually a chicken when it comes to dipping into the cold water here. But today, the ocean was calling my name. It tells me that it is time to be a kid again.

I had forgotten the little girl inside of me lately. I had forgotten how to be playful. I had forgotten what it was like to feel free. The little child within was feeling caged and was screaming to be heard. She needed to let off some steam. So I listened today, finally, and now I feel as if I'm being cleansed from my head to my feet.

I know I have work. I know I need rest. Now I must remember this…to keep the balance, I must have some playfulness.

Thoughts for Your Journey

If you allowed yourself, what would you do to be playful right now? Describe what you would do and then imagine yourself there. Set an intention for creating this in your life, feel as if it is already so, and give thanks to God for helping you create it.

Find time this week to indulge in some playfulness. Write about your experience. How do you feel? What emotions surface?

WHAT WOULD YOU LIKE TO ACCOMPLISH?

A giant sequoia tree lies before me. Its roots spring up from the dirt by at least ten feet. My girls and I are hiking through Sequoia National Forest. The day is absolutely inspiring. . .for more reasons than just its beauty.

My heart stops as Kolbi decides that she needs to climb the roots up to the trunk of this behemoth of a tree. From where she gets her desire eludes me. She's already tackled climbing many of the fallen giants, but this one is different. It gently slopes down a hill. I'm scared to death because I notice that if once upon the tree she decides to continue her trek, then she will find herself standing at least fifteen feet above me.

"Kolbi, please be careful." Fear takes over me. "I don't know if you should be climbing this one."

"Mom," Kolbi says as her face turns red, "do you not want me to do this?"

"Well, why do you need to climb this tree? It's not as safe as the other ones."

"Mom, I just need to know that I can. I want to know that I can do it."

And with that, I let Kolbi continue her journey. What an inspiration she is for me.

I need to know that I can, too. I have been asking myself why I need to write this book. I know in my heart that it is an avenue for me to find my truth and to give others permission to do the same. But what is my attachment to it? I haven't gotten an answer until today.

I need to know that I can. I need to know that I am capable of facing my fears. I need to know that I am capable of following through.

This fear has lingered with me for years. I dropped out of college, I dropped out of broadcasting school, and I never gave myself permission to live completely in my truth. So now I have to. My heart is screaming to let go of the fears. It is telling me that I have to trust that I can do it.

"Please, God, give me the strength to face my fears. Help me to believe in myself. Please show me the way to release the fear and pain. I'm handing it all over to you."

Thoughts for Your Journey

What would you like to accomplish in your life just because you need to know you can? What's holding you back from this? Ask the little child within.

Go within and ask God for guidance on how to attain your goal. First, ask God to move your fear out of the way for a moment so that you can get a clear answer. Then ask God for a message on how to begin. Remember, the message may not come right at that moment. It may be given through some other avenue. Just be aware and listen. What did you find for yourself?

FORGIVE YOURSELF

I forgave myself as a mother today. For the last thirteen years I have grieved over what kind of mother I was being. In my mind, I was never good enough. My whole world has been built on a picture that said I had to meet certain criterion to be a "good" mom. It was a picture in my mind that no human could attain. Well, today I finally let that picture go.

I took my girls out to lunch. We were having a nice time and as usual found ourselves having a little hen party in the bathroom. We tend to do that a lot. I began to reminisce about a time when the girls were one and three. Every time they climbed out of the bath they ran around the room in their birthday suits. Then they would hide in the cabinets so I could find them. Their bare little bottoms and chubby little legs will forever be ingrained in my memory as they giggled their way into their hiding places.

As these memories flooded my mind I made a mistake of sharing them out loud. "Mom, I asked you to please not talk about those things." My modest Mackenzie is appalled.

"Honey, I'm sorry. I thought you just didn't want me to talk about boys or anything personal now. This is when you were a baby. And, by the way, we are the only people in here. I'm not talking about this in front of anyone else."

"I don't care, mom. I don't want you talking about me like that."

I found myself getting angry. We headed to the car. Pictures of my life raced through my mind. For a moment there was silence. Then the emotions began to strangle me.

"I have lived my whole life for you kids. I have had nothing but you. You have been the center of my world and you don't even want me to remember it, much less talk about it. I am done!"

And in that moment I was. It was as if my whole world shifted. I knew right then that no matter how well I did my job as a mom, that my kids were going to choose to see it the way they wanted to. . .good, bad or otherwise. I knew in that moment that I could no longer work from a place of guilt and try to be the perfect mom. There is no such thing.

My mind shifted to my mom. "Oh, dear God, what have I done to her my whole life?" I saw how much guilt my mom carries because I chose during so much of my life to see her as the bad guy. It was my story. . .one that I created. In this moment of enlightenment I completely forgave her. I know that it's up to her to let go of the guilt and heal her life, but at least now I have released her.

I have finally released myself from this burden, as well. I can only be me. It's up to my kids and those around me to choose how they perceive me. I cannot control that. . .I never could. I just thought I could.

Ironically, I thought I had forgiven my mom a long time ago. I see now it has been happening in increments. I had to forgive myself as a mother before I could truly forgive my mom for what I perceived to be the mistakes she made with me.

We have to forgive ourselves before we can truly release those around us. We have to forgive ourselves for being human. We have to release the standards we've created for ourselves. Some of us try to reach them and feel as if we are always failing, and then some of us never attempt the challenge in the first place.

Isn't it funny that as we strive for a perfect picture of how we "should" be, that we are denying the perfection that we already are. The only perfection we will ever be is that of the spirit. I am getting one step closer by releasing myself today.

And that is why I continue to be on this journey. It is sometimes hard and it is sometimes emotional. And sometimes when I feel I am in a real dark period and don't know what's before me, I get scared. And then all of a sudden I see the light. I went through these last thirteen years of feeling guilty as a mother. But as I now know, in the darkness there are possibilities. There has been much happiness during this time, but overall there has been a darkness within me. But now the darkness is lifting. I have found true forgiveness. The guilt that was suffocating me is leaving. I can breathe. I see a light and the light is me!

Thoughts for Your Journey

Is there someone in your life that you are having a hard time forgiving? Ask yourself what is causing your pain. Is it because you haven't forgiven yourself? Write your feelings here.

Go to your meditation garden. Take a deep breath. See the person you are having a hard time forgiving in front of you. Imagine that person as a little kid. Ask this child what information he or she can reveal to you. If you have a hard time with this, remember, you can always ask God to take away the fear so that you can see clearly. You can also take this time to ask the person in front of you what is the gift you have given to him or her. What does the meditation reveal for you?

CELEBRATE EACH OTHER'S JOURNEYS

I ask myself why it is that I feel compelled to share what I've learned when someone else is telling me about a recent revelation. Why do I feel the need to toot my horn and let them know that I've already got the information? Is it because I feel threatened? I turn within to find my truth.

It is revealed that I just want to discover things for myself. And on this journey called life, each discovery is a celebration. I find that when someone else has made a discovery, I don't want him or her to talk down to me. I want them to honor me for my experiences on my own journey.

The other part of this is that I don't want to be left behind. I have been afraid that I didn't have enough information or wasn't smart enough. I have always had to convince myself, and others, that I am good enough.

I realize now I won't be left because when one person gets "the find," we all benefit from it. It's like man going into space. It may be just a select few going up there, but we all benefit from it. It's also like the great quarterback. He may seem like he's leading the way, but everyone on that team brings something to the table. They all make up the whole. Each one of them is needed.

We all make up the whole. I see now that I am just an archaeologist of the soul. I dig and dig to find my light. Others will benefit from my digging, but their greatest moments will be when they find their own lights.

We are all on a journey. Let us celebrate for one another as we make our own discoveries. Let us not pull each other down and take away those poignant moments. Let us all celebrate each other's moments of enlightenment, for we all are one. And when one of us makes a discovery, we all grow. For isn't that the answer. . .to be a part of the whole?

This truth sets me free. My whole life I wanted to belong, but always felt alone. I felt separate. The ironic thing was that the better I tried to make me, the more separate I became, because it was always at someone else's expense.

I am a person now who is the spirit first. And in that I celebrate each and every other spirit's discoveries as my own. For isn't my goal one of unconditional love for the human race. For every discovery made, our race takes one more step to wholeness, to love. I celebrate this and honor each and every person's journey. I no longer need to be right or first in these discoveries. I felt that way because of my ego. It has kept me in fear. But I can see that I am really starting to let it go. I am finally realizing that I am a part of the whole.

Thoughts for Your Journey

Are you able to celebrate others' journeys? Or do you "build up" yourself at their expense? Write your thoughts and feelings.

Draw a bunch of circles on a piece of paper. Imagine this as a group of people. Where are you in it? Are you a part of the whole or are you outside of it? What thoughts and feelings surface as you do this?

SURRENDER YOUR LIFE

It is a beautiful moonlit night. My friend, Renee, and I are at the beach. The power of the Pacific Ocean thrashes within twenty feet. We are following directions. . .not just any, but a message from God.

Last night Renee needed a healing. I am a spiritual coach and thus, I offered my assistance. As we began the healing, I asked for God to help me, to allow me to be a facilitator for Renee. I said my piece to her when all of a sudden the room filled up with the presence of God. Renee could not move at first. Then her body began to convulse.

"Terri, I feel like I'm throwing up and I can't stop."

Renee crawled out of her chair and lay down on the floor. She wept. She had been praying for a "jolt," as she calls it, to get her back on her spiritual path. Her prayers were answered.

I, on the other hand, was in shock. "Did this come from me? Did I do this?" My ego was playing games with me. The message I kept hearing was "Terri, this is for you. You need to let go and purge. Let Renee be a reflection to you as to what you need. Open your heart to the healing."

Renee came out of the healing with a new awareness. As for me, I was more confused than ever. "What was my part?" I asked myself this. My heart said, "Very little. You just held the space for the healing." My ego on the other hand said, "Wow! I'm really getting good at this."

Renee and I were both trembling. I knew in my heart something magnificent had just happened. I knew it wasn't me.

I always receive a healing upon giving one. How can I not with the love of God flowing through me? Well, this healing continued for me even through today. I wept and wept. God was trying to tell me that this was much bigger than I and for me to let go of all of the controls of my life, once and for all.

I called Renee. The tears continued to flow. Then I felt a presence above me filling my heart up with love. "Renee, please take a look and see what is happening to me." I was so muddled I couldn't see anything.

"Terri, there is an angel above your bed. It's telling you to go to the beach with me tonight at 8:30. We're supposed to bring a blanket."

"Okay," I said. I knew it was time for me to let go of the controls. I began to pray all day to let everything go. . .to let the tears of the past completely flow.

Then my sister Kelly called tonight. It was no coincidence. She's been on my mind a lot lately. Each time my girls fight, I think of her. Their battles remind me of my past. I wasn't the nicest big sister. I've held onto a tremendous amount of guilt because of this. Of course, our conversation led to our kids. I asked Kelly if she remembered me being mean to her as a kid. She said, "Yes. Yes, Terri. I just know that I spent many times out on our back porch swing crying because you had been so mean to me."

God was really working on me. All the barriers were coming down. "I am so sorry, Kelly. I am so sorry for having hurt you." I could barely get the words out through the tears. The purge was well underway.

It is now time for Renee and me to make our way to the beach. I am anxious for the healing. She is anxious because she is blind as to what she is supposed to do. This is new for her. She has to trust completely in the messages.

We spread out our blanket and I lie down. I pray to let my ego go and to open my heart completely up to God. Renee asks for guidance, too. With my eyes closed and my heart open, the spirit of God takes over.

In spite of a fight within me, I see darkness leaving. I weep, for I know I am finally letting go. At least that is what I think. Then I hear, "Terri, go bathe in the ocean. You need to do a final cleansing."

I begin to argue in my head. I do not believe that I am hearing a message from God. I argue that I have been sick for many weeks, that the ocean is way too cold and that I don't like the ocean at night. There might be sharks in there. I am too afraid. I convince myself that this is all just in my head. I am not trusting.

I think the healing is over. Renee and I begin to talk about it. I ask her if she received any weird messages. She explains what she saw. She saw the same as me. She describes the tug-of-war going on with my ego. I ask her if she was told that I should go into the water.

"Yes. Yes, I was told, but I didn't think there was any way, because you have been so sick. I heard it three times."

We sit there and laugh about it. Then a presence comes over me and once again I hear a message to go into the water.

"Renee, I have to go. God is telling me I have to go."

I stand up, wrap the blanket around me, and slip my clothes off very discreetly. I am afraid and, yet, I know it will be okay.

I make my way to the water. . .laughing and trembling. As my toes touch the water's edge, I hear, "Terri, you don't have to go in. You have finally surrendered."

I fall to my knees sobbing in thankfulness, in sadness, in happiness. All of the emotions are mixed into one. I am so thankful for seeing the power of God. I am sad for holding in so much pain for so very long. And I am so happy for having finally surrendered. I stand up and look to Renee. "I think I'm done," I say.

Renee looks at me with sternness and says, "Are you sure? I don't think so."

I fall to my knees. . .again. This is now a test in humility. People are running by on the beach. It doesn't matter. I am letting it all go. I have finally surrendered.

Thoughts for Your Journey

Are you ready to surrender the ego? You can do it now. Write your thoughts and feelings about this.

You can turn your life over to trust. It's up to you. All you have to do is choose. What's holding you back from this?

PRIDE VS. HUMILITY

Pride versus humility. The ego versus the spirit. They are one and the same. Quite honestly, I had not thought much about this until now.

"I am divine light. I am divine creativity. I am divine wisdom. I am divine love." This is my daily affirmation. I used to say, "God, please let me be a vessel for your love and light. Please, let me be a vessel of your wisdom." Then one day, it shifted. I heard during my prayer and meditation, "You already are these things. Everyone is. You just have to own it." And so I did.

But now a relative poses a question to me. She asks, "Are you not being prideful by saying that?" Well, I am not sure of the answer here so I go within to find out. I have no idea what I will hear. But I want to know the truth, even if it hurts.

My heart says that to be humble is to become a servant to God. . .to get out of the way with my ego. In other words, instead of controlling my life on what I think I should do, I must allow my heart to speak where God's messages come through. The message from my heart is my truth. It tells me that I was made to be worthy of all of God's love. And to be worthy of that love means that I can be a vessel of that love, if I choose to be. I choose to be a vessel of God's love, of God's divine creativity, of God's divine wisdom, of God's divine light. God has given us the power to be all possibilities. I choose to be a vessel of God's love and because God has made me worthy, therefore I am that vessel.

I am moving my ego out of the way and letting the power of God shine through me. I am divine because I am God's child. . .a living example of God's light. Therefore, I am divine wisdom. . .I am divine creativity. . .I am divine love. . .I am divine light. We all are!

Thoughts for Your Journey

Do you believe that you are a vessel of God's love and light? What thoughts does this journal entry bring up for you about pride and humility?

"Go within." It's time to have a conversation with God. Ask what is your truth. It's up to you to own it. You just have to choose.

TAKE GOD'S HAND, STEP BY STEP

As I take one more step on my journey, I find myself a little tired and a little frustrated. I'm tired of being sick and frustrated for letting it drag on. For the last six weeks I have been fighting a horrible cough. . .the doctor says I have a slight case of pleurisy. I know I have a big case of fear.

Fear has always manifested itself in me with either pain or illness. When my body hurts, it is like a barometer for me. It tells me something is not right. Whether it's telling me that I'm run down and need to clean up my life or telling me that I'm aching because of the emotional pain I'm holding inside, it is all because of fear. It is the fear of not facing my truth.

I have been in fear with my writing. I just recently began believing that this is what I am supposed to be doing, but I haven't been clear on where it is going. And since the ego likes to control things, not knowing where something is going is hard to stomach. So, as a result, I convinced myself that maybe I wasn't supposed to be doing it right now.

Messages that I should write have been sent my way for a very long time. That's how this book began. But in this last six weeks I've found myself in fear. I didn't know where this book would go. So I stopped myself and became frozen. I was waiting for God to give me some kind of signal. I was waiting for God to tell me what to do. Well, God did. It just wasn't the kind of message that I was expecting.

I had convinced myself that I would go along with life and then there would be this magnificent moment of enlightenment where God would tell me what to write and would lay everything out just perfectly for me. Wrong! I realize that my fear was playing this little game with my head. I became overwhelmed. I was looking at the end picture and not trusting in the path. I forgot that I was a partner in this endeavor and that it was up to me to dive into trust and to take a pro-active stance with this task.

Interestingly enough, I have continued to be pro-active in my daily healing process. I have been aware and I have been a co-partner in it and the enlightenment has been amazing. Just like when I had that beautiful experience at the beach when I surrendered. What I'm realizing right now, though, is that like anything else, "surrender" takes a time of integration, too. It takes time to manifest in all areas of your life. . .time to work its way through and through.

My lack of surrender with my writing froze me in a space where I haven't allowed myself to be a co-partner with this book as of late. Oh, yes, on occasion I have written an entry or jotted a few notes here and there, but there has been an overwhelming feeling of dread. I have been really scared.

Then I got sick. It started out slowly and the more I used the illness as an excuse to not write, the sicker I got. My heart tells me that I am grieving. . .grieving for all of the times that I have held myself back because of this kind of fear. It is trying to tell me through this illness that it is time to let go. . .to let go and let God take over.

What is my fear? My fear is that I'm not capable of seeing this book through, that the messages I've received to write this book have not been true. That is my ego talking. It's been getting in the way again. That's okay, though, because I have learned a huge lesson from it.

The lesson is this. If I stay in my ego, I am staying in fear. The two go together. On the other hand, if I let go and let the essence of God flow through me, then there is nothing to fear. This is just one more step toward surrendering. Like a child holding its momma's hand and learning to walk, if I take the hand of God and let it guide me through, step by step, then I can face the task at hand.

Thoughts for Your Journey

What parts of your life are still frozen in fear? How does the fear manifest itself?

Sit quietly with your inner child and go within. Go to that place of fear where you are frozen. Instead of fighting the fear, be with it. Let all of your emotions bubble up to the surface. Truly get in touch with what makes you so scared. With understanding comes freedom. Write what you have discovered for yourself.

GOD'S MESSAGES ARE EVERYWHERE

It is now about a week-and-a-half after what I call my "surrender" at the beach. It was this moment of surrender that allowed me to work through my fears of writing, showing me to take things step by step. It also gave me the strength to stand in my beliefs. The messages I hear are real. I am someone who needs to experience things. I can truly say that none of this is a figment of my imagination. I am a person who doesn't do well on blind faith. I need to see to believe.

I have learned through all of this that it is up to the person to heal. . .to open his or her heart. It's up to the person to feel the love inside.

I have also learned that everyone has a distinct way of healing that is unique to that person. We all have different paths. We each come into our spiritual truths in ways that are comfortable for us. Where one might call it Jesus, another might call it love. There is but one God.

I am so thankful that God is present in my life. I am slowing down enough to finally start listening most of the time. Yesterday, for instance, I was creating a class plan for a series of workshops. The words flowed through me until I got about halfway done. I then felt a little fuzzy. . .like I was being resistant or something. I was. I had gone into fear again. I was pushing to get through my work for fear that if I didn't get it done, it might never be finished. But this time, I listened.

I looked up at the clock. Earlier in the morning I had thought about taking an exercise class, but decided I had to work. When I looked at the clock and it was ten minutes before the class was to begin, I knew I was being told to get up and go. I did. It felt so good to follow my instructions. I still haven't finished my class plan and that is okay. It is unfolding before me just as God has planned.

I took Mackenzie and her friend Brooke to the mall yesterday afternoon. We were walking along eating some ice cream, when we passed by a bookstore. Out of the corner of my eye, something flashed at me to go inside. It was an angel guiding me. At first I ignored it. Then I made a quick turn on my heels and told the girls to come inside with me. I didn't tell them I had seen anything.

Once I walked in, I was a little confused. "God, what do you want me to see?" I turned around and looked straight at a magazine. It was *O, the Oprah Magazine* and in big letters on the front cover it said, "Trust Yourself." I started laughing. What a wonderful message for me. I bought the magazine, of course, and walked out of the store.

The girls and I stood outside of the bookstore for a moment when all of the sudden Brooke said to me, "Terri, that was so weird in there."

"What do you mean?" I asked Brooke.

"There were books falling off the shelves in there. . .for no reason. . .they just kept falling. We didn't even touch them." Brooke was a little overwhelmed.

I said, "Show me where you are talking about."

We ran back in. I probably don't even have to say this, but the books were right in the same area as the magazine. They were lightweight kid's books set up on a display. I guess God was making sure I was going to get the message and was drawing my attention to the right area.

Needless to say, when I shared with Brooke and Mackenzie what had really happened, they were amazed. Mackenzie was shocked a little less than Brooke, because she has seen so many things already. Brooke was so excited and wanted to know more about how to see. I told her you just have to be willing to open your heart for the healing and want to believe.

This brings me to today, where the messages continue. I was driving to the beach to take a walk this morning. Just as I was about to arrive I heard, "Terri, you really need a nap. Go home." I turned my car around and drove home, all the while questioning how in the world I would take a nap at nine o'clock in the morning.

When I got home, I crawled into bed and decided to read Oprah's magazine. Well, of course, there had to be a message for me. What article do I turn to? Miraculously, it was one on the importance of napping. I giggled with relief. Here was another message. I read the article and was reminded how important naps are for creativity. It said twenty to thirty-minute naps are best. So I put the magazine aside, I closed my eyes and said, "Dear God, I need a twenty or thirty-minute nap, please." But then I caught myself and realized that I was controlling this. So I said a different prayer. "Dear God," I asked, "please let me sleep as much as you think I need." I woke up three hours later.

So here I am now writing about this and feeling so much excitement about all of the possibilities. There are so many messages out there for us all to see. We just have to be willing to open our eyes and open our hearts for the healing. We have to ask and then be willing to receive. It comes in increments, small at first, tiny steps of trust. We have to be willing to trust in ourselves that we are worthy to receive these messages from God, that we are worthy of this kind of love. We just have to be willing to surrender and believe!

Thoughts for Your Journey

Do you believe these miracles can happen to you? Write your thoughts and feelings about this.

There are messages all around us. Go into awareness and ask God to help you see the signs. If you have a hard time with this and don't believe this can happen for you, then ask yourself this question, "What scares me about this?" Write your discoveries. Remember, you are worthy!

DETACH FROM THE OUTCOME

Boy, has my life shifted! I am so aware now of when I try to control things around me. But, instead of fighting it, I tell myself that this too will pass. I accept that it is just part of the process.

I taught a workshop last week. It was on powerful living. My workshops right now are what I would call "baby workshops." That's because I've been taking baby steps with them. Each one has been a great learning experience.

Well, last week's class was no exception. I prayed to get out of my own way and to let God's essence flow through me. It did. . .almost. The words that came were wonderful. I never knew what was coming next and then to my surprise words that were just perfect for the moment would come out. . .sometimes in a rhyme. I was blown away and thrilled that I had managed to get out of the way. I had surrendered!

When I left, however, something was not quite right. I checked in with myself and ran through the workshop in my head. I noticed that I had been watching the students to see if they were getting it. I was watching for a reaction from them. Were they crying? Were they moved? Were their lives being changed for good? I asked myself these questions. The answer that came to me upon looking at it was, "Aha! The good ol' ego is still intact."

But something funny happened this time. Normally, I work hard to figure out how to move the ego away. This time I didn't. I celebrated the fact that it had been brought to my attention. I asked what I was holding onto. The answer I received was that I was still attached to the outcome. I felt responsible. This time, however, I accepted it, for I knew in my heart that this too would pass. I surrendered to the process and truly accepted my humanness. As a result, the responsibility lifted.

This exercise in surrendering everything, especially responsibilities, has continued throughout this week. Mackenzie is now nine years old going on fifteen. She is extremely mature and has always had a mind of her own. When she was a year-and-a-half old she knew what she wanted to wear, her Little Mermaid outfit, and we had to make sure it was washed practically every day. Well, nothing has changed. Her will is even stronger now.

This week, Mackenzie informed me, "Mom, I like it when you're with me at home, but I want to live my own life when I'm doing things outside of our home."

At first, I was shaken by Mackenzie's blunt remarks. My friend, Linda, enlightened me. She has two college-aged girls. She advised me to listen to Mackenzie and to tell her that I trust her to make decisions from her heart.

This made so much sense. We already do this with A.J. I always tell him that I trust him. He's a wonderful human being. I just wasn't expecting to let go of the strings with Mackenzie so soon. A.J. is, after all, eight years older than Mackenzie. I thought it was my responsibility to make sure she was guided in the right direction. Well, the truth of the matter is, she already is heading in the right direction, if there is such a thing. She knows what she likes, how she wants to do things, and has strong convictions about many things. She is her own person. . .she is her own little unique being.

By talking to Linda, I saw my fear as the culprit. It was holding Mackenzie back and causing tension between the two of us. She was starting to resent me and dig in her heels during the times I thought I knew what was best for her, or the times that I didn't trust her thoughts on something. The truth of the matter was that I was acting out of my own past fears and not letting her discover her own.

So, today, in this space of surrendering and as I was discussing homework with Mackenzie, I caught myself worrying about the outcome again and my responsibility in it. I then turned around to her and said, "Mackenzie, I trust you. You have been doing such a wonderful job taking responsibility for your homework. I don't even have to say anything to you about this."

In that moment the world was lifted from my shoulders and the restraints were taken away from hers. Her huge smile said it all. She was on her own journey and so was I!

Isn't this what the journey is all about. . .trusting ourselves? As I trust myself to get out of the way and let go of the controls that determine the outcome of other people's lives and how it might reflect on me, it allows people to learn to trust themselves and be on their own journeys. What a relief!

Thoughts for Your Journey

Are you stuck in controlling the outcome of something in your life? Or have you surrendered? What thoughts arise for you after reading this?

Be with your discoveries. Give thanks for them. Try to accept that this is where you are right now and be in your humanness. Create an affirmation here that you can repeat to yourself when you go into fear and want to control. For instance, mine is: "I am divine light. I am divine wisdom. I am divine creativity. I am divine love." This brings me back into a space of love. Create something that rings true to your heart, or use the affirmation above if it fills you with love.

CELEBRATE YOUR LIFE!

I am ecstatic with my life and what's going on in it! Each day is a reawakening. I never know what to expect. I never know what the outcome is going to be about anything. And yet, I have never been so happy.

By taking the responsibility off myself to mold all of those around me, I am able to be the true me. I am not bogged down by what I might be doing wrong or what the outcome of my decisions will be. The guilt is fading away and so is all judgment. . .day by day. Because I have given the reins of my life to God's love inside of me, I no longer have to be in fear. I know that I just have to surrender myself to the process and listen. . .listen to the messages that guide me on my way. These messages of love are my truth, unique to me and no one else. We are all this way. We have our very own gifts to share with the world, if we just open up our hearts to our truths.

I am so excited about all the possibilities in my life. Never before have I felt this way. Because I didn't know what was around the next corner, I held myself back. I became frozen in fear, but not anymore. I am actually enjoying the fact that there are surprises ahead of me. I have no idea what my life has in store and now I celebrate that.

Life can be so much fun if we allow it to be. We are here to be in the process of finding our truths. . .the truth that abides deep within. . .the truth that tells us we are free. Freedom comes from releasing the controls of your life, and others', and finding a space of trust. This surrendering to trust takes you to a place of love and abundance. It takes you to a place of wholeness. . .a place where it is no longer "you against me," but a place known as "the we." Trust allows you to love and support those around you, but at the same time, lets them be on their own journeys. This is wholeness. This is love. . .unconditionally.

Thoughts for Your Journey

What's keeping you from celebrating the process of healing? Are you stuck in negativity? Are you still in blame? What's holding you back from living in all of your possibilities? What is your truth right now? Are you being truly honest with yourself?

You have a choice to let go. No one can do it for you. It's up to you. Let the presence of God surround your life and fill you up. There's no one holding you back. You are the one who has to open up to the truth. Believe this, YOU CAN DO IT! Write this: "I CAN DO IT!" and see how you feel.

THE POWER OF YOUR MIND

For the first time in my life, I truly feel like a winner. I went bowling tonight with my family and some friends. It was the first time that I can ever remember doing something competitive and not caring if I won. I just wanted to have fun. And did I ever!

When I first walked into the bowling alley, I felt those old jitters that told me the games were about to begin. You see, the games for me have been pretty much everything in my life up until I started to heal. The games were with myself and sometimes with others, but mostly with me. The games were filled up with negativity. They were the driving force in my head that told me I had to be the best. They were the mental games that always defeated me. It was a constant tug-of-war. It was all a part of my perfect pictures. . .my picture of how I thought I was supposed to be, but often times, ended in defeat. It was the ego at its best. It was how I defined myself.

This was the first time I had played something competitively in over a year. When I recognized what my mind and body were doing with this, I caught myself. And if I'm really honest, what I actually did was go to the ladies room and sat on the toilet. I calmed my body down, took some real deep breaths and checked back in with who I am right now, not in the past. I said my little affirmation, "I am God's light and I am God's love" and the fear went away. As a result, I had so much fun tonight because I knew my truth. My truth tells me that I am already a winner. . .we all are. Whether I win or lose a game doesn't define who I am. I finally get that. There is no need to play any more mental games.

It was interesting to watch the others playing tonight. I saw how they were affected by whether they were winning or losing. I asked one of the little girls who was with us how she was doing. She said she was losing. So I asked her if she was at least having fun and she said, "No, not really."

I used to be like that little girl. I couldn't celebrate just having fun. I allowed my negative thoughts to take over the controls. It always had to be a competition and I constantly dwelled on what I thought were my shortcomings.

When I look to the past, I see how I darkened myself with so much negativity. I held myself back. I had to be the best, but most of the time I wasn't. I hardly ever won, at least not in my mind. I was so stuck in negativity that I was never able to be the true me. I convinced myself that I was never good enough.

Well, tonight I made my thoughts positive ones. The power of the mind is vast. It can sink us in negativity or it can draw us to the light. We have to choose how to see things and then use the power of our minds to believe.

That's what I did tonight. . .I used the power of my mind to pull me out of the darkness and into the light. I reminded myself of who I am right now, not in the past. I put no expectations on myself, I bowled one of my best games ever, and most importantly, I had a blast!

Thoughts for Your Journey

You are already a winner! List at least five positive things you see in yourself right now.

Go out into the world and every time you find yourself being negative, go back to that affirmation you wrote earlier. Write a new one if you feel you need to. What are your discoveries? How does your awareness shift when you pull yourself back into the present moment with your affirmation?

Take a Leap of Faith

I took a great leap of faith today. I completely put my life and work in God's hands.

When I was stuck a few weeks ago and couldn't write, I wasn't sure where to turn. I kept looking for the signs. . .signs to show me how to handle my life. Then one day I was driving in the downtown area of our little town and saw a huge banner. It was for our Parks and Recreation Department. The banner said it was looking for teachers and lecturers. We have a wonderful program in our community for adults and kids. All of the sudden I heard myself say, "Why can't I?"

Boy, this was a shift for me. These are my husband's famous words. I asked the question and to my amazement, I felt no fear. So, I took the number down and made the call when I got home.

I am so thankful I made that call. I had prayed for quite some time for God to show me something or someone that could give me some guidance on my path. That call was the gift.

The man on the other end of the phone was so inspirational. His name is Idris. When talking with him, I felt as if I were speaking to someone like Dr. Deepak Chopra, one of the leading spiritual teachers and philosophers in the world, who is also a medical doctor and a best-selling author. Idris, it seemed, was my little gift from God.

We discussed ideas for classes that I could possibly teach in our community. Then Idris asked me to come down to City Hall and pick up some reading materials and paperwork to fill out. What came next was not what I imagined.

As I filled out all of the papers and proceeded with creating a lesson plan, I found myself getting sidetracked with this book. My frozen state was finally thawing out. As the days went by, and as I followed my inner truth and guidance, I found I wasn't really interested in creating the classes right then. I wanted to write. . . and so I am.

This is where the great leap of faith comes in. I called Idris today and said I no longer wanted to work on a class plan, at least not for right now. I explained to him how he had been a great gift and I thanked him for it. I told him I had to trust my messages and they were to master this plan first. . .to finish this book on my journey to wholeness. Then if it was a part of God's divine plan, we would find ourselves working together in the future.

Idris was wonderful and actually seemed excited for me. As for me, I'm excited, too. I am trusting in the path right now. Idris was my little gift to get me writing again. I trust that God has a plan for me. I don't have to be in fear. I don't have to be afraid that I've just cut myself off from teaching. If it is meant to be, it will be, one way or another, whether it's with our city or somewhere else. I'm trusting in the message and the message is this. . .God is guiding me!

Thoughts for Your Journey

Is there a particular place in your life where you would like to take a great leap of faith? Write your feelings about this.

Are you ready to take this leap of faith? Remember, there is only today. Tomorrow may not exist. God knows you can do it. I know you can do it. Now it's time for you to know it, too! What is holding you back from this?

RECOGNIZE PEOPLE'S PAIN AND FEAR

"Mackenzie, what are you afraid of?"

I ask my daughter this question. Her whole body is in fear and she is being very controlling. She is upset with her sister. Mackenzie has been bugging us for over a year to let her redecorate her room. She is nine and the last time it was done was when she was two. We've finally given her the okay and are letting her decide what she wants to do with the room. But now her little sister wants to copy her and is telling her what she wants to do with her room. Well, if you know siblings, this is taboo!

Mackenzie looks at me with a little shock. Usually when the girls get like this I ask them to leave the room. This time, however, the words just come from my mouth without thinking. This is one of the first times I can ever remember in a situation like this with my kids that words have shot from my mouth and not been judgmental. Usually I have to stop myself and think before I speak. . .but not this time.

I took Mackenzie by surprise with my question. She could tell I wasn't getting on her case or judging her. She knew I was trying to help. She felt my compassion for her. She's seen me in fear at times and we've discussed how it affects a person, how it makes them want to control the things around them.

"Mom, I want my room to be mine and I don't want Kolbi to copy it. I don't like it when people copy me."

"Well, sweetie," I replied, "you don't have to worry about that at this time. Kolbi just redid her room three years ago. It's your turn now. You can choose whatever it is you want to do. By the time Kolbi gets to redecorate her room again, she will not want the same as you."

And with that, the argument was over. It surprised me. I couldn't believe that simple little question would get to the bottom of things. But then, when I think about this, why wouldn't it? Isn't that the basis of everything? You either trust or fear. And when you ask the question, "What am I afraid of?" you often get an answer that leads you to understanding and trust.

What a huge moment of enlightenment for me today. I never thought of asking my kids this question. But it makes so much sense. By my asking the question and being an example of compassion to them and staying neutral with them, they can learn to understand themselves better. Before long they will be able to do it for themselves.

I'm so excited the power of God is working through me. I am really beginning to own these tools that I have learned. It has taken a lot of time and patience, but it's definitely been worth it. Because I am healing me, I find myself an example of "the we." Because I am integrating all of these lessons learned, they are becoming a part of me without my having to think. That's because I am finally moving out of the ego and working from the spirit. I've gotten me out of the way. . .at least some of the time. As a result, I responded with love and compassion for my girls today.

Thoughts for Your Journey

Be aware of yourself interacting with others today. See when they are in fear. Recognize their pain. Just "be" in this space of understanding and compassion. What do you discover about yourself?

After doing this exercise, did you find that you still have pain inside? See the reflection of the day. If you couldn't find compassion with someone in particular, then it's because you haven't found compassion with yourself in a certain area. What still hurts? Go within and talk to your little child inside.

CO-DEPENDENT RELATIONSHIPS

It's truly wonderful how trust makes a difference in your life. The other night, A.J. came in to talk. I was up late writing. He asked me what I was writing about and I told him "trust."

He said, "You know, Ter, I really appreciate how much you and Dad trust me now."

Remember, this is a seventeen-year-old telling me this. I am thrilled with his candor.

Then he said, "Sometimes, though, it's hard to watch you and Dad with the girls. It's so different from how you treated me."

"I know, A.J., and I'm sorry. But if we hadn't made a shift in our lives and started to heal, we wouldn't be treating them the way we are and we wouldn't be trusting you, either."

He nodded with understanding.

"You know, A.J., you and I are a lot alike. We both have a tendency to be a little stubborn and resistant."

He laughed at this remark. We both know this and talk about it often.

"A.J., I could have done things a lot differently with you, but I didn't know how. I learned a lot from you. I didn't like the way I was, and as a result, I decided to find a way to change. Now what's neat about that for you is, through my example, you can see it's okay to move out of resistance. . .it's okay to change. It takes great courage to do this. I never realized this until last summer. Now I know that I am courageous."

And with that he smiled. The seed had been planted just by having an open conversation. This nice little talk couldn't have existed if there wasn't already trust. A.J. knows that it's okay to make different choices in his life. He also knows that he is capable of doing and accomplishing many great things because we have trusted him. Because we have trusted him, he is learning to trust himself.

When we trust ourselves, we set an example for others to do the same. By watching us, they can learn to trust themselves. This is not just with our kids, but it is also with our spouses, our parents, our co-workers and our friends. I believe this is what some would call "breaking co-dependency."

I feel people create co-dependency in relationships by not standing in their own truths. Everyone is worrying about what the other thinks. They don't trust themselves to be who they really are. Some tend to blame everyone for what's wrong in their lives and want people to "fill them up." I feel some co-dependent people want others to validate them and take care of them. Or they feel they must give themselves up to make other people happy. They are in fear.

When someone decides to break that co-dependency as I did, then the people around them are forced to face themselves. For some, they take off running. For others, they choose to seek the truth.

That's what my husband did. Steve recently told me this. He said, "Terri, I feel better in my skin right now than I ever have. That's because you forced me to look at myself and depend on myself."

Now, obviously, I didn't force Steve to do anything. He weighs over 250 pounds! But what did happen was that I broke the co-dependency and he followed suit. He didn't have to. Steve could have run for the hills. He saw, though, how the changes were affecting my life and our whole family's for the better.

Don't get me wrong. . .Steve and I have had our moments. But, I can say, they were always a gift. Sometimes we didn't know it at the time and sometimes we wanted to strangle each other, but always there has been a gift. . .usually by getting closer because of a new understanding of each other. Where we used to argue a lot, now we seldom do. There is no need to, because there is no blame. No one is pointing a finger anymore. We both are trying to be responsible for ourselves and our own inner peace. We don't depend on each other most of the time to make each other happy.

Learning to trust yourself and stand in your truth affects everyone around you. Of course, there are those people who fall off by the wayside because they don't want to change. That's okay, too. We all have to make the changes when we are ready. . .not because we are forced to.

So, this is how trust works. I've never known joy and peace like this. . .not just within myself, but with my family, too. I feel as if I can handle anything that comes my way. I no longer feel that I have to know everything, be everything or control everything.

Trust has allowed me to be me and to break co-dependency. As a result, I feel my wings are expanding. I feel like I can fly. And the great thing about this, I don't have a clue as to just how high!

Thoughts for Your Journey

Are you holding yourself back from freedom because of co-dependency? Are you afraid of completely standing in your truth for fear that it's going to hurt someone else, such as a spouse, a co-worker, a parent, a child, or a friend? Are you afraid that it will take you out of your safety net? Go within and see if any of these things ring true for you.

What co-dependent relationship are you ready to release from your life? Do you trust yourself enough to take this giant step? Write what you feel about this.

Remember, the greatest gift you can give those around you is to break co-dependency and stand in your truth. By standing in your truth, the people around you are given permission to do the same.

BALANCE

Balance is one of the many benefits of moving into wholeness. For the first time in my life, I'm experiencing balance.

The need for balance was one of the biggest catalysts for my commitment to healing. I constantly found myself being totally obsessive about some things, while with others, I found myself completely shut down. But now, because I am finally listening to the messages and then acting upon them, I feel no need to struggle for balance anymore. It's just happening all by itself.

Because I got so stuck in guilt, fear, and judgment, my life was in chaos. If I allowed myself to be creative with something like heading a charitable fashion show, for instance, then I would be so obsessed with it that everything else in my life would suffer. And then if I got caught up in my kids' lives by feeling responsible for their happiness, at the expense of my own, I would get angry for having forgotten me.

Now, for the most part, I don't experience this anymore. I receive messages, guided instructions, every day through my prayers and meditations. All I have to do is listen and then follow them. It's called getting out of my own way and going with the flow. When I stay in the present moment and ask, "What is it I need to know right now?" and then follow my instructions, there is no room for doubt. There is no room for fear or judgment, because what happens is a space of love and a sense of balance.

I look back on all of the times when my life felt out of control. It was simply that I wasn't asking for guidance, listening, nor following my instructions. Now I find time to write, to be with my family, individually and as a whole. I find time to exercise and I even find time to take a nap on occasion. This balance is happening because I've surrendered, I'm listening, and I've let go of the controls.

Thoughts for Your Journey

What's keeping you from having balance in your life? Is there still too much on your plate? Are you asking for guidance and following it? Go within and talk to that little kid to find out what he or she needs at this time to create balance.

Begin your day by asking for guidance on what you need to do first. Then act upon it. After you have followed through, then do the same again. Try to keep your ego out of the way from telling you what you have to do or what you should do. Continue to follow through with this the whole day. Write down your discoveries.

We Are All Connected. . . Fear Keeps Us Disconnected

I am a clairvoyant. That means I can see and read energy. I see visions like movies. I didn't know I had this gift until I ventured on the road to healing my life. It scared me at first. It went totally against my beliefs. And then when I began to see God working through me. . .I knew I had to believe.

I just took my usual quiet time in the morning to meditate. I saw a vision that took me walking along a path of beautiful white light down a hallway. I found myself running down that hallway into a room filled with light. I came into the room feeling like I had arrived. Then I saw the most incredible, iridescent, brilliant golden light. It was the light of God. It stretched upward and outward for as far as I could see.

As I stood in awe of this magnificent scene, I noticed people walking out from the light. There was Jesus, there was my father, there were people representing all walks of life. Everyone was represented. . .the people just kept coming and coming.

As I continued to watch the people, I suddenly realized that everyone was filled with light and that from the tops of each of their heads they were connected to God's light. Every person looked to be a flicker of light from God's candle burning bright.

My attention turned to the fact that I could see everyone's physical bodies, but that the light that was within each of them also extended outwards to where there was no disconnection among the people. It was showing me that the physical body is all that separates us, but that the reality of our existence is that we really are one.

This oneness crosses all races, all religions. These are just different means to work out issues in our lives. . . to discover our truths. . .to discover that we all make up the whole, which allows us to feel free.

So now, as I sit here typing and sharing with you, I ask, "God, what else do you want us to know?"

I just took a moment of silence and this is the message I received. Everyone has the ability to see and feel God's light. My path of clairvoyance was just a way to discover it. Each and every person on this planet has his or her own path. The journey may be one of religion, it may come through AA, or it may come through walks with nature. It may come through work or it may come from play. These are a few examples of paths to take. It doesn't matter how you get there. What matters is that wherever you are, whatever you're doing, you must remember that you are a part of God's whole. You are the essence of God. It's now up to you to remember it. It's up to you to heal your life. It's up to you to turn to the love within and let God's light flow through you. You have a choice to heal. You have a choice to feel that you are a part of the whole. And like the vision revealed to me today, the truth is this. . .in spirit we are all connected. It is fear that keeps us disconnected.

God sent me a message one day. It said, "Fear creates separation. . .you against me."

Now I pose a question to you, "How do you choose to be, a part of the whole or disconnected?"

It's all up to you to be set free!

Thoughts for Your Journey

What keeps you feeling separate? Recall a recent memory when you felt disconnected from the world around you and write how you felt inside.

Become aware of your connectedness with or disconnectedness from others. Look for the moments when you start to feel separate. What fears are surfacing? Talk to your little child within. Understanding will help you move into a space of trust and wholeness. Write your discoveries.

REVEAL YOUR HIDDEN TRUTH

The truth shall set you free.

My journey guides me to new and different places, but with each stop, I reach a new awareness. I move into my truth. With each step, the chains of fear are released.

Yesterday, after I wrote that I was a clairvoyant, I got into the shower and began to shake. I had finally said the word "clairvoyant" in this book. I had been afraid to say this word for fear of the judgment I might face. I didn't feel strong enough in the past to stand in this truth, but now I do.

In our society there is a lot of judgment on clairvoyants and psychics. It's mostly because people are afraid of them and don't understand their gifts. I have even been accused of working with the devil. People have made these accusations without truly knowing me, or what I do. I have felt the judgment and for a long time I couldn't tell people that this was my work. This has been a deep-seated fear. And yet, my ability to see energy and understand people's emotions allows me to understand relationships and to help them when I can. It is all a gift from God. I'm just a vessel that God works through because I've chosen to open up to my truth. The irony of this is that everyone has this gift of the sixth sense. Most people don't want to own it, though, because of fear, so they judge and condemn it.

As I got into the shower and began to tremble yesterday, I looked back on how far I've come in owning my truth. It was just two years ago that Steve and I were in Big Sur for our anniversary. It was a beautiful day. We had stopped for lunch in an outdoor cafè overlooking the shimmering Pacific.

A family walked up to the table beside us. I noticed

their heavy southern accent. I'm still a southern girl at heart, being from Arkansas, and I can never resist saying hello to anyone with the sound of my home region's drawl. I had to ask where they were from and if they were on vacation. They had just moved to California from the Carolinas.

We enjoyed a very friendly conversation until the wife asked me what I did besides being a mom. I almost gagged. My throat tightened and the words would barely come out. I began to explain apologetically that I was a spiritual coach and that I try to help people discover their truths. Of course, she had to ask how I do that and I had to tell her that I am a clairvoyant. She didn't scream or throw things at me, thankfully. She actually seemed a little intrigued. I, on the other hand, wanted to make a mad dash back to our car and run as far away as I could.

"What is with you, Terri?" Steve was bewildered and stared at me as we went back to our car. "You were making me nervous in there by listening to you speak. Why were you so nervous talking about what you do?"

I knew Steve was right, as I had felt my whole body being in fear. I had to ask what I was afraid of and knew immediately that I didn't want anyone to judge me because of what I do with my life. I am different and was afraid that people couldn't accept me because of this. My whole life had been one of creating a "perfect picture" and this was shattering it. I also knew that this was my truth and that I had to let go of all judgments, mine included.

I can appreciate now just how far I've come. I have to confess, though, that I am still a little shaky. For quite some time, I've been able to speak this truth in California and with my friends, here and around the country, and with some of my extended family members. They are the ones who know what I stand for and accept me. On the other hand, there are a lot of people and family members that I haven't felt comfortable with sharing this truth. So for me to write this is taking it to a whole new level. . .a whole new level of acceptance of myself. It's just a little scary, so scary in fact that I had to stop writing a few moments ago and ask God to help me through my fear.

Claiming that I am a clairvoyant is really moving "out of the box." But it's my truth, and over and over, God has shown me that it is a gift. I use it to understand people. But nowadays God uses this gift to show me how to help empower others. . .to let them know that we all are worthy and that we all have gifts. We just have to step out of the box.

As I look back on my journey, I reflect on the night that I won the title of Miss U.S.A. Bob Barker asked me during the questioning of the top five contestants what message I would spread around the world to young people if I were to win. My reply was, "to be honest with yourself, because if you have honesty, then you have everything."

What courage it takes to be completely honest with yourself. It's scary. But it has to start somewhere. I thought I was completely honest with myself at that point of my life. I was honest to the point that my fear would allow me to be. I stayed in the box because I was in fear. . .in fear of being judged, in fear of being condemned. But staying in that box is what made me angry, bitter and resentful. So I had no choice. I either stayed that way or I had to delve deep within. . .deep within in total honesty. . .deep within facing my fears to discover my truth.

So, as I own my truth and come fully into who I am, I see that this is a step I must take. It is one more step to acceptance of myself. . .one more step to truly loving the person that I already am. . .one more step to wholeness.

Thoughts for Your Journey

What part of yourself have you disowned because of fear? What would you like to scream out to the world about yourself, but are afraid to do so? This is your chance to own this truth and be completely honest with yourself.

Take some time to go within. Feel the fear. Allow yourself to be in it. Take that little child within you and embrace him or her. What keeps you from revealing your hidden truth? Write your discoveries.

You Can Choose to be Free

"Mommy, there is something wrong with my heart. I'm not like the rest of the family." Kolbi's words are tear-drenched. Her little heart is aching so badly. She and Mackenzie had another fight and it ended when Kolbi pinched her big sister. I tell Kolbi that it is okay to be angry...we just need to find a better way for her to release it out of her body.

She is wailing now. "Mom, I can't stand it when people are always telling me what to do. Go to school! Get out of bed! And then Kenzie tells me when I can sing and when I can't. She says I can't do this and I can't do that. Even my friends tell me what I can't do. I hate it, Mommy! I hate it so much that my heart wants to hurt somebody! I feel like I want to run away sometimes, Mommy. I just want to be free."

Kolbi is boo-hooing. I know how she feels.

"Kolbi, you are a lot like me. Did you know that I used to hit people and throw things when I was mad?"

She is astonished, to say the least. But then she says, "Mom, I don't know who I am. All of the mirrors in our house look different to me. I don't even know what I look like."

My little seven-year-old is really deep. She overwhelms me.

"Kolbi, do you know how lucky you are? Do you realize how many people never want to know who they really are? You are so blessed to be you. You have a beautiful heart. You need to know that. I see you just the way you are in this mirror right now. You have beautiful blue eyes and beautiful blonde hair, and most importantly, you have a beautiful heart."

Kolbi finally smiles. She seems relieved because she doesn't feel so alone anymore.

I understand Kolbi's pain. It's horrible to feel the kind of rage she is experiencing. I have resorted to this kind of anger in the past, too. I felt controlled. I felt trapped. So, therefore, I felt the need to control what was going on around me.

I remember back to a time when I was a teenager. I took a knife out at my sister and told her I wished she were dead. In my freshman year of college, I put my fist through my boyfriend's kitchen window screen and was known to throw a few things. That same year my boyfriend had to pull me off of a girl I was pounding to death. She had said some bad things about my dad and I couldn't leave it alone. This was just a year prior to my winning Miss U.S.A. Those judges might have voted a little differently if they had only known that. There were even a few times in the beginning of my marriage when I was known to throw a glass or a slap. All of this anger stemmed from being in pain. . .from feeling as if I had no choice. . .from feeling I was being controlled.

But I did have a choice. We always have a choice to make. The other day, for example, Kolbi again was having a difficult time. This time she was feeling responsible for her dad's feelings again. This is an ongoing issue for her to work out. She cried because of the guilt she felt for not wanting to hang out with her dad at that moment. He was trying so hard to be with her and she just wanted nothing to do with him. Don't get me wrong, Kolbi loves her daddy and loves being with him. . .most of the time. On the other hand, she is resistant when anyone tells her she has to be with her dad. . .or anyone else for that matter. She likes being the "boss" of her own world. It's who she is.

Kolbi was really wailing. I pulled her into my arms. I told her that we couldn't change her daddy and that one of his big issues was the fear of rejection. I explained that he has a choice to heal this part of his life and that it wasn't her responsibility. I tried to enlighten her with the fact that we all are here to heal some kind of pain. Then I explained her part in this; she doesn't like being controlled. I shared with her that this is something she's here to work on and that I want to help her as much as I can. I told her that she has a right to feel like she does and that I don't want her to hold onto the guilt.

"Give me the guilt, Kolbi." I put my hand in front of her as if she could hand me something. "Come on, give it to me. No, how about I just take it."

So I acted as if I were taking a big chunk of guilt out of her heart. She grabbed it back and said, "No, I want to keep it." Then she pretended to swallow it.

"Kolbi, guilt can make you really sick. If you start holding onto the guilt now, then you will do it your whole life. It really can make you sick, honey. You may not see it now, but you will later on. I don't want you to feel that way and I definitely don't want you to get sick from it. You can choose to let it go."

Kolbi finally conceded and in the spirit of who she is, she said, "I'll do it myself." She then acted as if she were pulling energy out of her heart. "Mommy, it just keeps coming and coming. And it's all black and green and slimy."

Wow! I was so stoked. This is how I see guilt when I do healings. I actually see it as snakes. I never told her this for fear it was too gross and scary for her to hear.

When Kolbi finished removing her guilt, I taught her a tool I learned at Clearsight, the clairvoyant school I attended. I asked her to imagine putting her guilt into a beautiful rose, to send it out over the ocean, and then to blow it up like confetti. This is just a visualization tool to remove stuff out of our lives and to send it back to the universe with love. When she was done with this, I explained to her how important it is to fill herself up with God's light. . .to bring God's love in to fill up that hole. So she visualized a beautiful light coming from God that connected to the crown of her head and poured down flooding her space all the way to her toes. And with that she started to play.

Kolbi made a choice that day to heal. She is learning that she has the power to make choices. So, today, when she was screaming to be free and wanting to run away, I had to remind her of this again.

I waited until much later when she had calmed down. We were playing with our dog and then I said, "You know, Kolbi-bears, you said something today about wanting to be free. Well, honey, you can be. It's actually up to you to choose. You have to give yourself permission to be free. I am constantly telling you that you have a right to speak up for yourself to Daddy, to your friends, and to me. You are the one holding onto the feeling that you can't do that. You have a choice here. I can see you're doing such a great job of trying to speak up. You are doing it more and more. I'm so proud of you. I just want you to know that running away will not make these yucky feelings go away. You are the one who has to make the choice to set yourself free."

I probably said way too much here for a little seven-year-old's ears, but it's okay. I'm learning how to talk to these kids a little better each and every day. At least now, I no longer want to run away when something like this happens. That's because I am finally feeling free. That freedom rings throughout my soul because I made a choice. . .a choice to be free. . .a choice to be whole.

Thoughts for Your Journey

Is that little kid inside of you still feeling caged? What are you holding onto today that you can choose to release?

As you allow yourself to release the pain, ask what you need to learn from it and then visualize a beautiful rose in front of you. Imagine the darkness inside of you being pulled into the top of that rose, sort of like a vacuum, and then close it up. Now send that rose up to the sky, far away, and blow it up in your mind like confetti. Imagine a beautiful light coming down from God connecting to the crown of your head filling up your whole body and the space around you. Give thanks to God for healing your pain. What does this exercise reveal for you?

HEALING IS AN ACT OF LOVE, NOT AN ACT OF SELFISHNESS

My cup runneth over and it feels so very good.

When I first began this path of healing I was concerned that sometimes I might seem a little selfish. It was that societal programming again that says we always have to be giving. It's that programming that says you have to conform to fit in. I was fighting that battle within. . .to be the person I "should" be against the person I already am.

Well, I've discovered that the person I am is one of love, one of compassion, one of patience, and one of understanding. I never knew this until I took the time to get to know me. I was too angry in the past to see the good that was already inside of me. But now that I've stuck with my commitment to healing, I am in awe of how much there is to give. My cup is so full of love now because there is nothing to fear.

The fear is what kept me resistant to giving of myself. I had given so little to myself in the past that I wanted to hold onto whatever was left. I couldn't stand it when people wanted or needed my time or my patience. How could I give it to them lovingly, when I didn't even know how to give it to myself? How can a person love unconditionally when on the inside that person is full of pain and strife? It's not possible.

Oh, yes, you see some people give selflessly of their lives. But often when you ask them what it is that they need or like, they can't answer you. They have no idea of their truth. If they would just take time to get to know themselves, then they might discover they've tapped into only a fraction of what they are capable of.

That's how I was when it came to living powerfully.

 Message Sent 233

Many people told me in the past that I was so powerful and so capable of doing anything. I felt only an inkling of what they were telling me. I didn't know my truth. But now I do.

I know that I am capable of giving love like I've never known. Where I used to want to scream at my kids and even had visions of running away, I don't anymore. I now send love to their pain.

And when someone is rude to me, I no longer feel that I have to take the blame. I find my heart is full of love and compassion for them where there once was hate.

And when life seems like it's starting to get a little tough, I now know there is no need for panic or fear. . .I just turn to trust.

This is love. This is where my heart is. I didn't know it could be this good. I've found a love within that is so full I can't help but let it overflow to those around me. I am finally being that light that I asked to be. As the saying goes, "Ask and ye shall receive!"

Thoughts for Your Journey

What things have you discovered about yourself that you like, but weren't aware of until you began to heal? Write each of them down and tell how you feel.

What are you manifesting in your life right now? Are you experiencing more love and compassion? If for some reason you are still holding yourself back in certain areas of your life and don't feel you are seeing much change, be okay with this. Have compassion for the little child within. Acceptance and forgiveness of where you are right now is the true key to wholeness.

STOP TRYING SO HARD

I am so overwhelmed by the power of God. . .it is a power so much bigger than I.

I have felt for the last month that this book soon would come to an end. That is the message that has been sent to me through my meditations and prayer. I just didn't know how it would end. At this point, I am still not sure.

All I do know, though, is that God is preparing me. The first message came a few weeks ago after yoga class. I met a woman who has published children's books. She gave me a few words of wisdom about having a strong belief in what I've written and not sharing it with anyone until I feel it's ready.

I went to have my car washed this week. I picked up a *Learning Annex* magazine. It tells about classes being offered in the Los Angeles area. What did I turn to? Well, as you might guess. . .two different classes on publishing books.

That same afternoon I had lunch with a former Miss Universe from New Zealand. Lorraine published a book recently in her home country. It is no coincidence that this was the first time in sixteen years I had talked to her and now she was here to tell me the dos and don'ts of publishing.

With all of this information coming at me, I felt the need to push ahead. . .to get to the end. Then I went into effort. You see, in the past, we're talking many years ago, procrastination was my middle name. I would put things off out of fear, sort of like this summer when I got stuck in my writing. But in the past I was like that all the time. The only way I ever got through anything was if I had a deadline.

When I started my healing journey, fear took over again. Only this time it was by being in effort. I was trying too hard. I wanted to push ahead on my path. I tried to get all of the answers before I was ready for them, wanting to make sure that I didn't get stuck again.

This is what happened today. I found myself trying to write. . .trying to get to the end. I tried to force the words to come out, but there was no coercing them. They wouldn't budge. And for a moment I found myself in fear. "What's next? What should I do, God?" I asked these questions, but sat without an answer.

I decided to leave the writing until later. I had to give it over to trust. I was presented a magical, wondrous gift as a result.

I went shopping with Mackenzie and some friends. In search of her ideal vision of what a Halloween costume should be, we found ourselves at a weird little store I had never been to before. I made my way through all of the craziness to look up and see a familiar face.

"I know you," I said to the man in front of me.

"Yeah, you're Ball's cousin. . .aren't you?"

I had met this man two years ago through my cousin, Steve, who was visiting from Georgia. This man, Bob, and I talked a lot that night about our different philosophies. I haven't seen him since.

"Hey, how's your writing going?" I asked him. I remembered that he talked about writing something that night. I just couldn't remember what it was about.

"Well, I got my book published."

"How did you do that?" I was blown away. God works in mysterious ways.

Bob and I exchanged numbers after a little chat. He suggested a book for me to read on publishing. I couldn't believe the miracle that was being put before me. Just an hour before this I had been in fear. . .in effort. And now look, once again, at what was happening. God was showing me that there is a plan. I just have to be willing to be in trust, letting the almighty power lead me by the hand.

Thoughts for Your Journey

Are you in effort right now? Are you procrastinating about something in your life? Or are you working from a space of trust? Spend some time with yourself and write down your feelings.

If you are not working from a space of trust, what's keeping you from it? Go within and talk to that little child. Embrace him or her and feel the fear that is inside. Allow your body to release the pain. Let the message be revealed to you. Write down any thoughts or feelings that surface for you.

EMBRACE THE WHOLE YOU

What is the gift that resides in you? What is your truth? Are you starting to see it yet? Do you believe that you have a gift? Well, you do. We all do.

I never believed that I had a gift of any kind. I felt as if I did a lot of things pretty well, but nothing that stood out in my mind. But by opening up my heart to the love inside, I have discovered that I do have something to offer.

I am not special. I am no more important than anyone else. Just because I see visions and hear messages from God does not mean that I am better than you. I believe that I am writing this book because God wants you to know that you can have this, too.

Everyone has the ability to see and hear the messages. Everyone has the ability to converse with God and the beautiful angels that surround us. Everyone has a gift to share. You just have to choose to believe and choose to heal.

You must first start with your intention. This works for any of life's situations. Visualize a picture of how you would like to see yourself. Imagine that you have already created this as a reality in your life and are completely living it. Celebrate it in your mind and allow the feeling to take over you. Then give thanks to God for having received this healing.

Move into an awareness so that you may receive the messages that are there for you. At first you may be resistant to believing the messages. I was. Accept this. It is part of the process. Allow your little miracles to happen. "Own them." They are your beginning steps to wholeness.

Give yourself permission to be human. Forgiveness is the key. There is no sense in holding onto past guilt...it's debilitating.

Release all blame. See the gift in each situation. By looking at life this way, you can see your reflection.

Your responsibility to the world is to heal. That's it. You are not responsible for other people's paths. Nor are you responsible for their happiness. All you can be is a light unto the darkness and fill your cup so full that the love floods over to the world around you.

Embrace the child within. Give that little inner voice your consent to speak. Love that little child and see him or her as unique.

Be authentic. Stand in your truth. Release others' opinions as the authorities in your life. Turn to trust and let God be the guide.

And finally, take time each day to be thankful for all of the gifts you have received, because even in the darkness, there are many possibilities.

So, in the essence of gratitude, I would like to thank you now for all of the help you have been to me. This leg of my journey is coming to a close. God only knows what the future holds and it is so exciting. All that matters is this present moment, this space in time. And that is why I must say thank you. You have allowed me a voice. . .a voice that has set me free. Thank you for sharing my journey in discovering the true me!

Final Thoughts for Your Journey

Who are you? What do you believe about yourself? Do you believe there is a gift inside of you? Are you ready to express this truth to the world around you? If you still have reservations about expressing who you are, then ask, "When I go to my deathbed will I have any regrets?" Take some time and think about this.

Own your truth. Grab it. It's yours. Right now, in this moment, I want you to write your truth. Not what anyone else thinks, but what you feel. . .what rings true to your heart. You have the power to choose right now. There's no holding back anymore. This is it. Go for it!

In Closing

I am weeping. Only this time, the tears are of joy. I did it! I can't believe I faced my fears, finished this book and now stand in my truth. No words can describe this feeling I have inside. I have never felt this way before.

God sent me a message to find the love within. So, I opened my heart to trust and to the love of God and I faced my fears. I let God guide me by the hand, taking me step by step, into a place called love.

I feel my insides exploding with delight. Instead of the angry volcanic eruptions of the past, I am filled with God's divine light. I didn't know it could be this way. . .this fullness I feel inside.

Responsibilities to the world around me kept me caged. But now I feel free. That's because I have forgiven me.

I had to forgive myself for not being the perfect picture of how I thought I "should" be. This perfect picture told me to keep my voice inside, to conform, and that I wasn't good enough to be loved simply for being me. These responsibilities said that everyone was more important than the little child within me.

I thought I had to make everyone happy at the expense of neglecting me. I thought I had to strive and strive and always achieve so that people would accept me. But just as with winning Miss U.S.A., this didn't make me happy. That's because I denied the true me.

I finally accept my humanness. I don't have to "fix" me. All I need to do is allow my light to shine through... the light that got buried beneath the pain of the past.

This is me. I have owned my truth. My cup feels so full. I can see it overflowing all around me. I find myself wanting to give back to the world, with no fear of getting lost in the crowd. I have discovered compassion and understanding for the world around me. The love inside abounds.

And so I thank you once again for traveling this journey with me. You are a beautiful light, a source of inspiration. Because of you, I forged ahead to find my truth. I knew before I could feel love for the world around me, for you...I first had to find it within myself. No longer does it have to be about "me," because I finally feel a part of "the we." I feel whole, and it feels so good. Thank you... thank you.

—Terri Amos

Also available, a companion CD,
Message Sent, Meditations for Retrieving the Gift of Love.
For further information, to purchase CD, or to contact
Terri Amos for speaking engagements,
please go to **www.terriamos.com.**